Dear Melba 9/29/11
Thank you for
your genuine friendship
with my
mother
over the
years.
In Christ's
Love,
Laura

BIRD'S-EYE VIEW
of the BIBLE | EACH ONE TEACH ONE

by Jean Eason & Orpah Hicks

D0823098

COVER DESIGN BY PHIL KIDD.
The three olives represent the Trinity.
The 12 olive leaves represent the 12 apostles.

Unless otherwise indicated, all Scripture quotations
are taken from the New King James Bible.

BIRD'S-EYE VIEW OF THE BIBLE
Copyright ©2010 Tutors for Christ
Library of Congress Control Number: 2010921780
ISBN 978-0-578-04896-3

Published by Tutors for Christ
467 Sandalwood Dr., Lexington, KY 40505
www.tutorsforchrist.org

Printed in the U.S.A.

Dedication

We dedicate this book to our children and grandchildren. We pray that these pages will not only present a bird's-eye view of the Bible, but it is our heart's desire that as you grow in your personal relationship with God you will find love, peace and joy.

Acknowledgements:

We have used a number of Dr. David Reagan's articles from his web site: www.lamblion.com. We appreciate the biblical research he's done. Dr. David R. Reagan has 20 years of experience in teaching international politics with 30 years of teaching and preaching the Bible.

He is founder and director of Lamb & Lion Ministries, a non denominational ministry. He serves as the host of the ministry's nationally broadcast television program called "Christ in Prophecy." He is the author of 8 books.

We wish to thank Betty Stephens, Peggy Legg, Vanda Weathers and Tammy Moore for meeting with us weekly, giving helpful insights as well as making corrections.

Also thanks to Bill Hylton, our editor,
Pat Cobb, our proof reader,
and Laura Doolittle, our designer.

Jean Eason and Orpah Hicks
Lexington, KY
www.tutorsforchrist.org
jeaneason@windstream.net
samhic@windstream.net

CONTENTS

The Purpose of this Book

- To give you a bird's-eye view of the Bible. Many volumes have been written explaining the foundational truths of the Bible. We've tried to make these important subjects easy to understand.

- To emphasize the importance of developing a personal relationship with God – He loved the world so much that He sent His son, Jesus, to redeem mankind.

- To understand God's absolute standards - God has given all humanity commandments that clearly differentiate right from wrong. Nothing can be compared to God's wisdom.

- To increase your knowledge of God's Holy Word. When you regularly study the Scriptures and commit to prayer – your life will be changed as significantly as the testimonies in the last chapter of this book.

- To impact your life and encourage you so much that you'll want to read it with one or more persons. Or perhaps a group of your friends would like to meet weekly for about an hour to read each chapter. This is truly the way lasting relationships are formed and acquaintances become friends; however, it's the work of the Holy Spirit Who brings the conviction of truth.

- To encourage evangelism teams calling on people whose names have been given by the congregation. After a nine-week Bible study one gains more insight into Christianity's teachings. It could also be useful in mentoring as well as including it in "new member welcome packets."

Preface

In this day and age, one can turn on the computer and google any word under the sun and instantly find a ton of information. In fact, with all of the modern technology and TV news, there is hardly any subject that the average person is not aware of.

When it comes to seeking relationships, a person can be on the computer chatting with someone across the ocean and yet has never talked to the person next door. Families can hardly have a conversation without being interrupted by someone texting or the cell phone ringing. Where will it end?

With everyone's busy schedules and multi-tasking, there is little time for family discussions and just sitting quietly listening to other people's ideas and opinions. All too often people can be in the same household, all doing their own thing – never talking to one another.

People Have Questions

In spite of busyness in our lives, most people still want answers to important questions. How did life begin? Why do we have to die? What happens to me when I die? Is there life after death? What should be my focus in life? Where can I find answers – is the Bible true? Do all roads lead to heaven? What is the truth? Does God really exist? Where can we find answers to these questions?

The Bible has an answer to these questions. It explains why we have good and evil, sickness and death. It gives hope for the future and how you can find comfort. God really does care about you! Humans have a need for truth. This truth is found in the Bible. Obviously, truth is not something humans can imagine or invent on their own. Only God Himself is the source of truth. Only He can make truth understood and satisfy the emptiness in people's lives.

There are Absolutes

We cannot determine how much time we may have left on this earth. No one knows that! Sickness, accident or death can come at any time – then what?! You are here in this world and that's an absolute fact. How you arrived has not changed and some day you will die. There are some things in this world that we cannot deny. The birth of humans and animals has not changed. It has always been and always will be as long as the earth exists. Months, years and seasons continue to pass – the sun, moon and stars continue to shine – trees, grass and flowers continue to grow – and every person and every creeping creature continues to die.

I just don't know what to believe.
How can I know who is right?
Do all roads lead to eternal life?
Where do I begin?

CREATION

Truth

The Path to GOD

Worldview

CHAPTER 1

Why Believe the Bible?

At some given time in our lives, we ask these questions and more! For thousands of years, Christians have relied on the Bible to supply answers to the needs of life. The World Book Encyclopedia states that the Bible is an ancient *reliable* manuscript. The Bible itself claims over three thousand times to be the revealed Word of God. Christians believe the Bible is God's gift to you and me. Let's look at some reasons why!

The Bible is different from any other book

[2] It is unique among books. It contains sixty-six books with continuity of theme and purpose. The biblical authors speak on hundreds of controversial subjects with harmony and continuity from beginning to end. There are at least forty different authors, who wrote on three continents, in many countries, and in three languages. Among these authors were kings, farmers, lawyers, generals, fishermen, ministers, a tax-collector, doctor, some rich, some poor, – thus touching many experiences of men extending over 1500 years, covering forty generations. It tells how mankind's problems began and how they will end. It is an unfolding message of "God's salvation of mankind." And best of all, it tells about the conclusion of this world and the beauty of a new world where we can all live in peace with no more sickness, sorrow or death.

[3] The Bible is a book that has no equal. No one has been able to disprove any biblical claims. Many critics have attempted to discredit the Bible. Three well known writers who held

---

1-2 What do Christians think about the Bible and why is it unique?
      What were some of the backgrounds of biblical authors?

3 Has anyone tried to disprove the Bible?

atheistic or agnostic views; C.S. Lewis, Josh McDowell and Lee Strobel, were converted to Christianity in their pursuit to disprove the Scriptures.

The Bible is Historical

[4] Did you know that there are hundreds of historians who have affirmed the accounts in the Bible? One notable Jewish historian, Favius Josephus, (37-100 A. D.) is the author of Jewish Antiquities. This is a twenty volume history of the Jews from their beginnings to the close of Emperor Nero's reign. It records hundreds of detailed events of Jewish history that appear in the Bible. In the preface of one volume, Josephus said, "Now I have undertaken the present work, as thinking it will appear to all the Greeks worthy of their study; for it will contain all our antiquities, and the constitution of our government, as interpreted out of the Hebrew Scriptures." Imagine – the constitution of government out of the Hebrew Scriptures!

[5] The Bible itself explains that much has been written about the events of that time that could not be contained in the Bible. The rise and fall of many Israelite kings is recorded in I Kings (979 B.C.) Here are just a few: King Nadab (I Kings 15:31); King Baasha (I Kings 16:5); King Elah (I Kings 16:14); King Jehoshapat (I Kings 22:45). The New Testament (N.T.) also addresses the same subject: *"And there are also many other things that Jesus did, which if they were written one by one, I suppose that even the world itself could not contain the books that would be written"* (John 21:25).

The Bible is scientifically accurate

[6] Science is the observation and study of the world around us. The Bible is not a book on science; however, where it men-

---

4 Who was Josephus?

5 Were there other books written about kings mentioned in the Bible?

6 How does science agree with the Bible?

tions creation, (science) it speaks accurately and without contradiction. For example - Isaiah 40:22 mentions the "circle of the earth," a clear reference to the roundness – not flatness of the earth. One of the reasons God created the sun, moon, and stars was to be for signs, seasons, days, and years. Through scientific study we have learned the accuracy of the "circle of the earth."

One rotation around the sun is a year
One rotation of the moon around the earth is a month
One rotation of the earth is a day
Sailors navigate using the skies as a compass

Who can look into the sky day or night without wondering how it all began? The Bible says, *"… God has created these things."* (Isaiah 40:26) *"The heavens declare the glory of God; and the firmament shows His handiwork"* (Psalm 19:1).

[7]It's truly amazing how God created the earth as evidence of His love for us. Everywhere we look, we see the fingerprint of the Almighty God! (Romans 1:19, 20). As good and amazing as all this is, God did something even more astounding – he made mankind the pinnacle of all his creation. In fact the Genesis record states that we are created in the image of God (Genesis 1:27). Does this not make us *very special*?!

Archeology supports the Bible

[8]Archaeology is the science of investigating and recovering remains of past cultures. It involves the study of architecture, language, literature, art, tools, pottery and many other items that have survived the ravages of time. Archeological discovery doesn't confirm spiritual truths but it shows the Bible is historically and geographically accurate. Sir William Ramsey, a celebrated British Archeologist and former atheist, became a Christian upon

---

7 Who is the pinnacle of God's creation?

8 How does archeology support the Bible?

discovering the Bible's amazingly reliable archeological record. For almost two hundred years, those who study biblical archaeology have been working in the Middle East in their quest to recover the past. There have been thousands of archaeological finds that have advanced the study greatly, but some are more significant than others. These finds are interesting from an educational point of view and do validate the historical accuracy of the Bible. Some of these finds have been the Dead Sea Scrolls, the Crucified Man, and the Pilate Inscription. Let's briefly look at each one of these to see why they are significant.

Dead Sea Scrolls: The Dead Sea Scrolls discovered in 1947 contain approximately 900 documents and fragments. The scrolls predate 100 A.D. and include a complete copy of the Book of Isaiah. The significance is the age of the documents and the astonishing lack of variants. About 99% are punctuation or spelling errors. Incredibly, none of the variants changed the meaning of the text, nor did they contain any significant theological differences. This gives us the assurance that the text we have today in our Bible is the same as the early church had two thousand years ago.

Crucified Man: This is the remains of a full skeleton of a man crucified in the first century. The foot bone contained a bent crucifixion nail. There have been those that argued that the crucifixion of Christ was a hoax because that was not a form of capital punishment in Christ's time. These remains verify that crucifixion was being done and that the crucifixion of Jesus was done exactly as outlined in the biblical narrative.

Pilate Inscription: This stone tablet was found in the theater of Caesarea and bears an inscription mentioning the name of Pontius Pilate, the procurator of Judea, and the Tibe-rium. This was an edifice, built by Pilate in honor of the Emperor Tiberius. There has been much written to discredit the biblical narrative in regard to the existence of Pilate. This tablet clearly says that it was from "Pontius Pilate, Prefect of Judea" and verifies that he was a person that lived during the time of Jesus, as written in the biblical narrative.

For more information on archeology: www.gotquestion.org

The Bible is Prophetic

[9] Prophecy is pre-written history. The Bible has over 8300 verses that contain predictive prophecy making a total of over 700 prophecies. Prophecy that has already become history pro-vides strong motivation to believe the other prophecies of Scrip-ture that remain to be revealed. Fulfilled prophecy and the laws of probability constitute evidence of the Bible's authenticity as a product of divine intelligence.

[10] Is there a chance that later writers 'fudged' these prophecies by writing them, or re-writing them, after the events occurred? No, because the ancient hand-written scrolls were copied and distributed far and wide. No one could possibly have collected all the copies, from Egypt to Babylon, to make such later modi-fications. And enough copies have been found, nestled among ancient artifacts unearthed during archaeological digs, to estab-lish that they were written long before the events they accurately predicted.

[11] For example, consider the prophecies of the nation of Israel when they were obedient: *"That in blessing I will bless thee, and in multiplying I will multiply thy seed as the stars of the heaven, and as the sand which is upon the sea shore; and thy seed shall possess the gate of his enemies; and in thy seed shall all the nations of the earth*

9-10   What is significant about Bible prophecy? Why is it not likely that Scripture was fabricated, making it seem that prophecy was fulfilled?

11   How did God deal with Israel when they were obedient ?

be blessed: because thou hast obeyed my voice" (Genesis 22:17, 18).
[This was locally fulfilled in their conquest of the Promised Land
(Israel) but it will also be universally realized in their global rule
during the Millennial Kingdom. (See chapter 2)

[12] And notice God's punishment when they were disobedient: *"The Lord will scatter you among all peoples, from one end of
the earth to the other..."* (Deuteronomy 28:64; see also Leviticus
26:33). This was fulfilled after the destruction of Jerusalem by
the Roman Empire in A.D. 70. The survival of Israel since 1948
is a testimony to God's faithfulness to His promise that *"He who
keeps Israel neither slumbers nor sleeps"* (Psalm 121:4).

[13] Dr. David Reagan's study includes 108 Old Testament
(O.T.) prophecies, including time and place of Jesus birth, that
were fulfilled at Jesus' first coming. The following are a couple
of examples of Old Testament prophecies:

> **Foretold in Old Testament:** *"But you Bethlehem, though you
> are small among the clans of Judah, out of you will come for
> me one who will be ruler over Israel, whose origins are from
> of old, from ancient times"* (Micah 5:2). NIV [predicted 700
> years before the event]
>
> **Fulfilled in New Testament:** *After Jesus was born in Beth-
> lehem in Judea…Magi from the east came to Jerusalem and
> asked, 'Where is the one who has been born king of the Jews?"*
> (Matthew 2:1, 2). NIV
>
> **Foretold in Old Testament:** *"Therefore, the Lord himself will
> give you a sign: The virgin will be with child and will give
> birth to a son, and will call him Immanuel"* (Isaiah 7:14).
> NIV [predicted 700 years before the event]
>
> **Fulfilled in New Testament:** *"But the angel said to her, 'Do
> not be afraid, Mary, you have found favor with God. You will*

---

12 How did God deal with Israel when they were disobedient?

13 Name some prophecies in the O.T. that were fulfilled in the N.T.

be with child and give birth to a son, and you are to give him the name Jesus. He will be great and will be called Son of the Most High. The Lord will give him the throne of his father, David, and he will reign over the house of Jacob forever; his kingdom will never end.' 'How will this be,' Mary asked the angel, ' since I am a virgin?'" (Luke 1:30-34). NIV

[14] The Bible alone is the only "holy book" that contains fulfilled predictive prophecy. There are no detailed prophecies in the Koran (Islam's holy book), the Hindu Vedas, the book of Mormon, or the sayings of Buddha. The Bible gives a strong warning regarding false prophets (Deuteronomy 18:21). **For more information on prophecy: www.lamblion.com**

Human Government is rooted in the Bible

[15] The U.S. founding fathers mutually understood that *"rights and freedoms"* are a gift from God and not bestowed by a king or government. The roots of *our judicial system* are in divine law. A carving of Moses holding the Ten Commandments stands center front over the entrance to the Supreme Court building in Washington, D.C. To most of America's Founding Fathers, the Bible was true, and it was the only source upon which to establish the new, independent nation. It's important for every American to understand what they knew to be true - that America's freedoms are based on Christian principles and that only a widespread Christian faith and general belief in God could keep our freedoms secure is easily seen in the declaration of independence: *"We hold these truths to be self-evident, that all men are created equal. That they are endowed by their Creator with certain unalienable rights that among these is life, liberty and the pursuit of happiness."* (Declaration of Independence, 1776)

---

14 What does Scripture show concerning the coming of Jesus in the Old and New Testaments?

15 How did the founding fathers feel about their rights and freedom?
    According to the Supreme Court, (1776) where did our judicial system stem from?

[16] Take note of a unanimous decision made by the U.S. Supreme Court commending and encouraging the use of the Bible in Government-Run Schools.

"Why may not the Bible, and especially the New Testament... be read and taught as a divine revelation in [schools] - its general precepts expounded, its evidences explained, and its glorious principles of morality inculcated?. . .Where can the purest principles of morality be learned so clearly or so perfectly as from the New Testament?" [Vidal v. Girard's Executors 1844]. Again we can hear this same wisdom from the U.S. Supreme Court five decades later: *"Our laws and our institutions must necessarily be based upon the teachings of the Redeemer of Mankind. It is impossible that it should be otherwise; and in this sense and to this extent, our civilization and our institutions are emphatically Christian"* (U.S. Supreme Court, 1892).

[17] As you can see, our government was built on biblical principles. Even though our human government is far from perfect, it has served us well; the function of human government is to govern the human heart and man's behavior. Jeremiah 17:9 says, *"The heart is deceitful above all things and desperately wicked; who can know it."* (also Mark 7:20-22)

The Bible can help us cope with personal problems

[18] God is a God of love and desires to reach our minds and heart. He reveals truth in every avenue of our lives, including personal problems. The book of Proverbs provides much counsel and instruction. We read, *"Trust in the LORD with all your heart, and lean not on your own understanding; in all your ways acknowledge Him, and He shall direct your paths"* (Proverbs 3:5,6). This book was written many centuries ago, yet it speaks to mankind today about vital subjects such as:

16-17   Discuss America's freedom according to the Supreme Court in 1844 and 1892 ('appendix A)

18-19   How can the Bible help us cope with personal problems?

gaining wisdom
  parenting
    immorality
      dishonesty
        wickedness
          drunkenness
            envy
              anger
                laziness
                  hopelessness

[19] It shows how to search our hearts and reveals the importance of not allowing the wrong kind of pride to exist in our heart. It also teaches us how to pray, manage disputes, settle finances, and have good relationships with others. The Bible's principles apply to all people of all nations and its counsel is always beneficial. *"Thus says the LORD, your Redeemer, the Holy One of Israel: 'I am the LORD your God, Who teaches you to profit, Who leads you by the way you should go"* (Isaiah 48:17).

[20] **TALKING POINT:** The Bible does not seek to prove the existence of God. It simply states that He does exist. Hebrews 11:3, 6 says, *"By faith we understand that the worlds were framed by the word of God, so that the things which are seen were not made of things which are visible," "But without faith it is impossible to please Him, for he who comes to God must believe that He is and that He is a rewarder of those who diligently seek Him."*

[21] Think about this: What if forty people who are not acquainted with each other are given a piece to a puzzle and invited to bring their puzzle piece to a dinner. At the dinner when their individual puzzle pieces are assembled they fit perfectly, forming a complete picture. How could this possibly happen?

20-21   Discuss the analogy of the puzzle.

Would this not be confirmation that their puzzle piece and invitation to the dinner came from the same person? Who other than God could touch forty authors with varied backgrounds on three continents over a period of 1500 years covering forty generations, bringing about such a book as the Bible?

[22] Christians believe the Bible is God's gift because it provides answers to life's complex questions. For them, it shapes beliefs, values, and lifestyle decisions. It provides comfort, love and support and leaves no room for doubt that a God of love has prepared a wonderful future for life after death. It is an absolute fact that we will all die some day. What lies ahead for you? You will be encouraged to learn about the New Heavens and the New Earth in the next chapter.

22 Name some reasons why we should believe the Bible is God's Word.

OK! Maybe the Bible is true —
so what? I have no desire to
go to heaven and float around
on a cloud! What is God's
plan for mankind?
Where is heaven?

CHAPTER 2

A New Heaven and New Earth
The Second Coming of Jesus

Well, who in their right mind would want to float around on a cloud forever and ever? But what if you knew you could live in a beautiful, perfect world where you would experience:

perfect love and peace —
  perfect health —
    perfect relationships —
      where even the animals would be at peace?!

²No doubt you would say, "That would be heaven on earth!" Well, believe it or not, God has made such a promise: *"Now I saw a new heaven and a new earth, for the first heaven and the first earth had passed away. Also there was no more sea"* (Revelation 21:1). Yes, God will restore his original plan for mankind! *"For behold, I create new heavens and a new earth; and the former shall not be remembered or come to mind." "They shall build houses and inhabit them; they shall plant vineyards and eat their fruit. They shall not build and another inhabit; they shall not plant and another eat; for as the days of a tree, so shall be the days of My people, and My elect shall long enjoy the work of their hands"* (Isaiah 65:17, 21, 22) Can you imagine living in such a beautiful place?

God's Plan
³God created Adam and Eve to live forever in a perfect world. He gave them everything that people enjoy. He wanted to share

1-2 What does the Bible say about a new heaven and new earth?

3-4 Why did God create the earth in the beginning?

His beautiful creation with the humans he created and enjoy fellowship with them. God's desire was for them to have dominion over everything that moves on the earth: *"And then God said, 'Let Us make man in Our image, according to Our likeness; let them have dominion over the fish of the sea, over the birds of the air, and over the cattle, over all the earth and over every creeping thing that creeps on the earth." So God created man in His own image; in the image of God He created him; male and female He created them. Then God blessed them, and God said to them, "Be fruitful and multiply; fill the earth and subdue it; have dominion over the fish of the sea, over the birds of the air, and over every living thing that moves on the earth"* (Genesis 1:26-28).

[4] God's beautiful creation declared His awesome glory and He would be glorified when mankind took dominion, carrying out His intention for humans to occupy the whole earth and reign over it. Imagine how this dominion could have produced societies that would glorify God! Imagine humans exercising their God given creativity and intellect, using their skills to benefit culture and all that exists.

Why don't we live in a world like that today?

[5] God provided everything for the first humans, Adam and Eve, to enjoy. All God required from them was *to follow his plan – obedience is essential!* He only gave Adam one warning, *"And the LORD God commanded the man, saying, 'Of every tree of the garden you may freely eat; but of the tree of the knowledge of good and evil you shall not eat, for in the day that you eat of it you shall surely die"* (Genesis 2:16, 17). God did not want Adam to know evil, but he gave him free will — the ability to choose. Unfortunately he made a wrong choice and he lost his privilege of living forever in a perfect world. And so it is today. Each of us are:

---

5 What was the one and only requirement God gave Adam?

descendants of Adam
> living in a fallen world.

[6] Each of us has a choice to make every day between good and evil. Things usually go well when we make right choices. *"Blessed is a man who perseveres under trial; for once he has been approved, he will receive the crown of life which the Lord has promised to those who love Him"* (James 1:12 NASB). Evil came into the world when Eve:

listened to the enemy,
> made the wrong choice, and
> > enticed Adam to eat the forbidden fruit.

Adam chose to listen to Eve and disobeyed God. Who was this evil one who brought sin into the world? This will be discussed in another chapter.

[7] Because Adam and Eve made the wrong decision and listened to a voice other than God's, justice was demanded. *"Then to Adam he (God) said, 'Because you have heeded the voice of your wife, and have eaten of the tree, of which I commanded you, saying, 'You shall not eat of it:' cursed is the ground for your sake; in toil you shall eat of it all the days of your life; both thorns and thistles it shall bring forth for you; and you shall eat the herb of the field. In the sweat of your face you shall eat bread, till you return to the ground; for out of it you were taken: for dust you are and to dust you shall return"* (Genesis 3:17-19).

Disobedience demands justice

[8] So now you know where justice began. If someone harms you or your family in any way, you want justice! If we violate the laws of the land, society wants justice. If we didn't have a judicial

---

6 Do you think obeying God is important?

7 How were Adam and Eve punished for their disobedience?

8-10 What brought death to mankind? Did man have a choice?

system and your family member is murdered, or someone harms you, what would you do? Without laws of justice, we would have chaos! Justice demands punishment for the one committing the crime.

⁹ The first human act of sin is documented here and punishment was carried out. What other explanation can be given as to how mankind has lived for the past six thousand years, knowing good and evil? God will not, however, allow evil to prevail forever: *"And the* LORD *God said, 'Behold, the man is become as one of Us, to know good and evil: and now, lest he put out his hand, and take also of the tree of life, and eat, and live forever' – therefore the* LORD *God sent him out of the garden of Eden to till the ground from which he was taken"* (Gen. 3:22, 23). By putting them out of the garden, they could no longer partake of the tree of life! We have inherited their sin nature, resulting in death, but God has revealed His future plan for a new heaven and new earth, a marvelous plan for obedient mankind.

¹⁰ God is a righteous, Holy God – he did not punish Adam without a warning: *"…for in the day that you eat of it you shall surely die."* Not only did they die in God's day, but hardship came with it. They had a choice to obey God and have eternal life in a perfect world, or disobey and die.

The earth was made to be inhabited

¹¹ Even though the first human beings failed, God will restore His perfect world. He did not create the earth in vain. *"For thus says the* LORD, *Who created the heavens, Who is God, Who formed the earth and made it, Who has established it, Who did not create it in vain, Who formed it to be inhabited: 'I am the* LORD, *and there is no other"* (Isaiah 45:18.) *"The earth will abide forever!"* (Eccl. 1:4).

---

11 Will God restore His original plan for mankind?

12 How does Isaiah describe life on the new earth?

Life on the New Earth

[12] We read where people will build and inhabit their own houses on the new earth (Isaiah 65:17). Imagine a perfect life where even the animals would be at peace with you! *"The wolf also shall dwell with the lamb, the leopard shall lie down with the young goat, the calf and the young lion and the fatling together; and a little child shall lead them. The cow and the bear shall graze; their young ones shall lie down together; and the lion shall eat straw like the ox....they shall not hurt nor destroy in all My holy mountain for the earth shall be full of the knowledge of the LORD as the waters cover the sea"* (Isaiah 11:6-9).

[13] The plant and animal life will similarly be transformed back to its original perfection before the curse. The result will be incredible agricultural abundance: *"'The days are coming,' declares the Lord, 'When the reaper will be overtaken by the plowman and the planter by the one treading grapes. New wine will drip from the mountains and flow from all the hills.'"* (Amos 9:13 NIV)

[14] The prophet Joel adds that *"the threshing floors will be full of grain, and the vats will overflow with the new wine and oil"* (Joel 2:24). The implication of these passages is that Man will no longer have to strive against nature because weeds and poisonous plants will cease to exist and rainfall will be abundant. In fact, Isaiah tells us that areas of wilderness will be transformed into glorious forests (Isaiah 35:2) and deserts will become *"springs of water"* (Isaiah 35:7).

[15] He is going to make all things new, and we are going to live in perfect bliss in the New Jerusalem (Revelation 21:5). (Psalm 2:8; 96:10) The Almighty God will then be the glory of His people forever and ever! (Isaiah 60:19-22).

[16] Abraham looked forward to living forever in a city (Hebrews 11:8-10). Jesus gave His followers a promise of preparing a place

---

13 How does Amos describe animal and plant life in the new earth?

14 Will man strive against nature?

15-16 Who will make all things new? What did Abraham look forward to?

for them (implying permanence) (John 14:2). Take note of how New Jerusalem is described by Dr. Reagan in the next section.

New Jerusalem – by Dr. Dave Reagan

[17] All my life, while growing up in the Church, I was taught that the Redeemed would live eternally with God in Heaven. One of the most amazing discoveries I made when I started studying Bible prophecy is that the Redeemed are not going to live forever in Heaven. Rather, we are going to live on a new earth, and God is going to come down to that earth to live among us.

[18] The Bible is very clear about this. Read Revelation 21:1-7. The only way you can get around the conclusion that the Redeemed will live eternally on a new earth is to spiritualize the new earth to mean Heaven. That is exactly what many Bible interpreters have done, and there is no justification for it.

[19] John says in Revelation 21:1, *"I saw a new heaven and a new earth."* What happens is that God burns up the old earth. We're told in 2 Peter 3, that He will burn away all the pollution of Satan's last revolt. He will take this earth and reshape it like a hot ball of wax, and out of that fiery inferno will come the new heavens and the new earth, an earth that will be refreshed and beautified and perfected to what God originally created before it was polluted by sin and changed by the curse (2 Peter 3:10-13). It will probably be greatly enlarged because it is going to serve as the foundation for a gigantic city — the New Jerusalem.

[20] Just think of it! As God creates that new earth, we will most likely be suspended in the heavens inside the New Jerusalem watching the greatest fireworks display in the his-

---

17-19 What will happen to our present earth? Will the new earth be larger?

20-21 Where is New Jerusalem before it comes to earth? What does Rev. 21:2 say?

tory of the cosmos. And when it's all over, and the earth is refreshed and renewed, then the Lord will lower us down to the new earth inside the New Jerusalem (Rev.21:2). We are going to live eternally inside that glorious city located on the new earth.

[21] That's right; the Bible never teaches that we will spend eternity in Heaven. It teaches that we will spend eternity in new bodies in a New Jerusalem on a new earth, and it further teaches that God will come down to that new earth and live among us: *"I heard a loud voice from the throne, saying, 'Behold, the tabernacle of God is among men, and He shall dwell among them, and they shall be His people, and God Himself shall be among them"* (21:3). He's going to wipe away every tear from our eyes, and there will no longer be any suffering — no pain, no death, no sorrow (21:4). He is going to make all things new, and we are going to live in perfect bliss in the New Jerusalem (21:5).

The Size of the City

[22] The incredible size means the city would stretch from Canada to the Gulf of Mexico and from the Atlantic coast of America to Colorado. It would also extend 1,500 miles into the atmosphere.

[23] This tremendous extension of the city vertically into the air is a clue that the new earth may be considerably larger than the current earth. Otherwise, the city would not be proportional to its surroundings.

[24] Would such a city be able to adequately accommodate all the Redeemed? That's a good question. The best answer I have ever run across is the one provided by Dr. Henry Morris in his book *The Revelation Record*.

22-23 What can we compare the size of New Jerusalem to?
       How does it compare with the current earth in size?

24-25 Is it reasonable to believe all of the redeemed could live in New Jerusalem?

[25] Dr. Morris postulates the total number of Redeemed might be as many as 20 billion. He further guesses that approximately 75 percent of the New Jerusalem might be devoted to streets, parks and public buildings. Can 20 billion people be squeezed into only 25 percent of the space of this city?

[26] The answer is yes! In fact, it can be done easily. Each person would have a cubical block with about 75 acres of surface on each face. We are talking about an immense city!

[27] This assumes, of course, that our new glorified bodies will be immune to the current law of gravity, as are the bodies of angels. This is a safe assumption, for Philippians 3:21 says that our glorified bodies will be like the body of Jesus after His resurrection, and His body was not subject to gravity, as evidenced by His ascension into Heaven.

[28] This is the reason the city will be so tall. We will be able to utilize and enjoy all levels of it. There will be vertical streets as well as horizontal ones.

The Beauty of the City

[29] And what streets they will be! The Bible says they will be "pure gold, like transparent glass" (Revelation 21:21). In fact, the whole city will be made of pure gold with the appearance of clear glass (Revelation 21:18).

[30] The city will sit on a foundation made of 12 layers of precious stones (Revelation 21:19-20). Each layer will feature the name of one of the 12 apostles (Revelation 21:14). The city will be surrounded by a jasper wall over 200 feet high (Revelation 21:17). There will be 12 gates, three on each side, and each one will be named for one of the tribes of Israel (Revelation 21:12).

26-28 What is the estimated acreage for one person? What is the reasoning for glorified bodies?

29 What will the streets be like?

30-31 Describe the appearance of the city.

[31] And yes, the gates will be *"pearly gates,"* each one consisting of one huge pearl (Revelation 21:21).

[32] Best of all, God the Father and Jesus will both reside in the city with us (Revelation 21:22). The Shekinah glory of God will illuminate the city constantly, and thus there will be no night nor will there ever be any need for any type of artificial light or the light of the sun (Revelation 22:5).

[33] The throne of God and His Son will be in the city, and "a river of the water of life, clear as crystal" will flow down the middle of the city's main street with the tree of life growing on both sides of the river, yielding 12 kinds of fruit — a different fruit each month (Revelation 22:1-2).

[34] That's it. God's Word only gives us a glimpse of Heaven. But what a tantalizing glimpse it is! It's a glimpse of perfect peace and joy and beauty. **Recommended reading: Heaven by Randy Alcorn.** —WWW.LAMBLION.COM

What happens when you die (we do not cease to exist) – will be discussed in chapter 4. Would you like to make reservations to live in this New Earth? Read the next chapter and find out how.

---

32 What will be the best part of the city?

33-34 What will be in the middle of the city? Is this a glimpse of heaven?

Gee, I had no idea of a New Heaven
and New Earth. At the moment,
I have no plans for life after death —
so how do I make reservations?

CHAPTER 3

Making Reservations

All of our lives we make plans. Our parents planned our schooling. After school it was time to grow up — find a job, a place to live, perhaps get married and start a family. But who plans for life after death? Sadly, too many neglect to do so. *Now* is the time to plan because you never know when your life will end. You just read about the wonderful new world God is planning for His children. Did I say, "children?" Yes, that is the number one requirement for making reservations. You *must* become a child of God.

² We also learned that God's original plan for Adam and Eve was to populate the earth and live forever in the perfect world He had created. We learned that Adam and Eve's disobedience separated them from God; therefore, each of us are born with a sinful nature, separated from God (Romans 5:12). Adam and Eve would have lived forever, but due to their sin, they brought physical and spiritual death to themselves and to the rest of mankind. We don't like to think about death — but it's a fact that you and I will die someday. No one escapes death! Scripture tells us there is life after physical death. We do not cease to exist. In order to live forever in God's presence, we need to clean up our act — we need to do something about our sin problem in order to become a child of God (Romans 3:23).

What is sin?

³ Sin is falling short of God's expectations and His purpose for our lives. The foundational core of the human race — the very

---

1 Have you planned for life after death?

2 What separated Adam and Eve from God?

3 What is sin?

basics that make up human behavior, the uniqueness of the individual's life and all that he is — is summed up in the Old Testament. It is the historical record of how God dealt with the human race since the beginning of time. It describes the details of:

His blessings and covenants,
　　His requirements for obedience,
　　　　His statutes for law, order, and justice,
　　　　　　His warning and punishment and
　　　　　　　　His requirement for sin sacrifice.

[4] The first prophecy in the Bible is recorded in Genesis 3:14,15. God promised humiliation and defeat for Satan. But victory over sin would be accomplished through the coming Savior Who would be crucified. Bible chronology names the descendants through whom the Savior was born (Matthew 1:1-17), the One who would take care of our sin problem. Jesus fulfilled the first prophecy and He promised to come again someday.

Good and Evil

[5] What is good and what is evil? Who is to say that evil is not good? For example, who said it was wrong to murder someone? And who should bring justice for the crime?

Justice — where did that come from? What would life be like if justice wasn't demanded? When we run a traffic light, ignore stop signs, steal, get involved with pornography, commit acts of violence and don't pay our taxes — what happens? We would live in a world of chaos, if there was not law and order. Who established these laws to begin with? God!

[6] Justice demands punishment for wrong doing. What happens when parents do not carry out punishment for disobedient children? The children suffer — they do not learn discipline and

───────

4　What is the first prophecy recorded in the Bible and who does it address?

5　Who brought justice, law and order into the world?

6　What would happen if we had no punishment in our world?

will grow up being dysfunctional. When society carries out punishment for wrong deeds, it carries a warning to others. God's justice was shown to Satan, *"So the LORD God said to the serpent: 'Because you have done this, you are cursed more than all cattle, and more than every beast of the field; on your belly you shall go, and you shall eat dust all the days of your life"* (Genesis 3:14)

Freedom of Choice

[7]After the first humans sinned, God said, *"And the LORD God said, 'The man has now become like one of us, knowing good and evil. He must not be allowed to reach out his hand and take also from the tree of life and eat, and live forever.' So the LORD God banished him from the Garden of Eden to work the ground from which he had been taken"* (Genesis 3:22-23). Their eating the forbidden fruit opened their eyes to knowing good and evil. This is the beginning of man's knowledge of knowing right from wrong. They made the wrong choice. Justice was declared – death was brought into the world. Had Adam made the right choice they would have known good only.

The First Murder

[8] The first murder was committed by Adam's son, Cain, who killed his brother, Abel. God said to Cain *"If you do well, will you not be accepted? And if you do not do well, sin lies at the door. And its desire is for you, but you should rule over it"* (Genesis 4:7). God knew Cain's heart. Does this not clearly say that God wants us to rule over sin? The entire conversation is not recorded here, but no doubt Cain knew how to be accepted by God! Perhaps Cain was jealous of Abel.

[9] It's obvious that Cain did not have a repentant attitude (Genesis 4:6,7). When God asked Cain where his brother was,

---

7 How did Adam and Eve come to know good and evil?

8 Who committed the first murder? What does Genesis 4:7 say about sin?

9 What was God's attitude about the murder?

he said, *"'I do not know. Am I my brother's keeper?' And God said, 'What have you done? The voice of your brother's blood cries out to Me from the ground'"* (Genesis 4:9-10).

[10] Since the beginning of time, every society has had to deal with human frailties of sin. But God did not leave us stranded. He planned from the beginning to take care of the sin problem by sending His Son to earth (Isaiah 9:6). His name would be Immanuel, which means, *"God with us."* (Isaiah 7:14). Clearly, all who recognize Jesus as the Messiah recognize that something amazing happened when Jesus appeared on the scene. Mankind needed a Redeemer (Isaiah 59:2) because man could not save himself.

The Sin Solution

[11] Then the time came for God to send His only begotten Son into the world to offer Himself as a sin sacrifice for mankind once and for all (I Peter 1:18-25). The birth of Jesus Christ (Luke 2:8-12) was absolutely unique among all births in human history. The birth itself was a normal human birth, but His conception (Mathew 1:18) was altogether miraculous. Mary was a virgin (Matthew 1:23) – God planted the divine "Seed" in Mary's womb, free from any inherent sin-nature and from any transmitted mutational defects, *"as of a lamb, without blemish and without spot"* (I Pet 1:19).

[12] Jesus became a part of His own creation, and shed His blood on the cross (Matthew 27:32-40). Was this not a great act of love and mercy for all? (John 3:16). What manner of love is this – for Jesus to give up His heavenly home and come to earth to show the glory of the Father and die for the sins of mankind (2 Corinthians 5:21).

[13] As Jesus went through the country-side performing mighty miracles that only the Creator could do, He demonstrated His

---

10 What does Isaiah prophesy? Why do we need a Redeemer?

11 What amazing thing happened that changed history? (Appendix B)

12 What can we understand from what Jesus did on the cross?

supernatural power over nature, sickness, and disease (Matthew 8:14-17, 23-27; 9:27-31; John 11:38-44). He raised the dead and cast out demons (John 11:38-44; Mathew 8:16). A sinless man died on the cross, and paid the ransom cost – he bought back what Adam lost (I Timothy 2:6).

Recognizing Our Personal Sin

[14] When we have children, it doesn't take long to recognize that they are born with a sinful nature. Have you ever wondered why one of the first words a child learns to say is, "No"? Why do they need to learn obedience? Why does each of us *need to learn* the difference between right and wrong? Clearly, the reason is because we were born with a sinful nature. Do you recognize sin in your life? Many of our sins are a result of things that have happened to us during our life time, such as erroneous teaching, neglect, rejection, and abuses of all kinds. We've all developed our individual habitual ways of thinking, feeling and behaving. We can get a good idea of what sin is by reading the Ten Commandments (Exodus 20:1-17). All wrongdoing is sin, but all can be forgiven (I John 1:9). Once we come to understand that we *do* sin, and are separated from God *because* of our sinfulness, Jesus' earthly mission of bringing forgiveness is very good news (John 3:17). What a marvelous thing Jesus did for us by paying our sin debt!

Following Jesus

[15] In the New Testament, we see a pattern of belief and action that people followed whenever they were coming to Jesus. As Jesus and the disciples traveled from place to place, many became believers and followed Him. They recognized Him to be the Son of the living God and they saw how He healed the

---

13 What did Jesus demonstrate and what is a ransom?

14 How do we overcome sin? Where can we find a good idea of what sin is?

15 How was Jesus recognized by His followers?

sick and lame. They heard Him preach and believed He came to not only show the glory of the Father, but also pay their sin debt and offer them eternal life. They recognized Jesus' love and appreciated His teaching them about the Kingdom of God. We become followers of Jesus in a similar way (Romans 10:9,10; Mark 16:16).

Can you believe in Jesus?

[16] Most people are familiar with the verse, *"For God so loved the world that he gave his one and only Son, that whoever believes in him shall not perish but have eternal life"* (John 3:16). Some people will respond by saying, "All you have to do to have eternal life is believe in Jesus? That's too easy!" This is because they are speaking in terms of intellectual knowledge.

[17] There's a huge difference between intellectual knowledge and "heart" (relationship) knowledge. The word "believe" in this verse means one has become convicted that the person of Jesus truly is the Messiah (Matthew 16:16), divinely appointed author of eternal life (Acts 2:14-41). They recognize Him to be the way, the truth and the life (John 14:6) and they desire to have Him in their life. They want Jesus to be their Lord and Savior (Romans 10:9,10). It's like a person when they become engaged — they have fallen in love and desire to be united with that person for the rest of their life. Like leaving the single life, and entering into marriage, the new believer confesses his sins and is buried with Christ in baptism to walk in newness of life (Romans 6:4).

You are now making a "U-Turn"

[18] After repenting of your wrong deeds (Acts 3:19,20) you will have a new beginning. This means you'll turn away from the things you know are wrong. When you truly agree with God

16, 17   What does it mean to "believe in Jesus? (Appendix C)

18   What does "repent" mean? Can we "earn" eternal life?

about what is right, your behavior will follow. It's like driving a car, it goes in the direction in which we steer it. It's up to each of us to decide which direction we'll take. When we choose God's direction and drive away from our sinful life-style by repenting from being on the wrong course, we make a "U-turn." Repent means turning away from the things you know are wrong. Can you begin to imagine what a wonderful gift Jesus gave when He died for our sins? And just think, you don't have to lift one finger to earn this gift — it's free! (Ephesians 2:8,9). By receiving Him in faith (John 1:12) you become His child and you can rejoice in the hope of the glory of God (Romans 5:1,2). You know how it feels when you've been working all day in a dirty environment and then take a shower — you feel so clean and refreshed! That's how you feel "spiritually" when you repent and invite Jesus Christ into your life. You have been spiritually cleansed! But this time, you feel clean *inside*, as well!

A New Life in Christ as His Child

[19] Scripture describes new believers as new creations (2 Corinthians 5:17) because they have been spiritually reborn and have a completely new relationship with God. You will still have a lot of the old life, but it is now going in a new direction. Things change as we grow and mature over the course of our lifetime (2 Corinthians 3:18).

[20] As we grow in Christ we are like children who need nurturing, training and knowledge in adapting to our new spiritual life. At the moment of salvation we enter a completely new relationship with God. He becomes our Heavenly Father and we, His adopted children. Suddenly we have a totally loving, patient, understanding Heavenly Father who never threatens us with guilt or fear. He accepts us unconditionally because Jesus has paid

19-20 What kind of change takes place after we become a child of God?

for all of our sins. As we come to know Him better and absorb these truths, we become less fearful, less guilty, more confident and more fully alive. This can bring about radical changes, but like an adopted child has to get acquainted with his new parents, it takes time for us to get to know our Heavenly Father. That's why we need to study the Bible, pray and fellowship with other Christians. We increasingly enjoy the wonders of our relationship with Him. That, in turn, begins to change our personalities. It enables us to feel more secure, forgiven and free. This, in turn, helps us connect and be more understanding of others.

Jesus, Our Example

[21] Jesus is the most emotionally, spiritually and relationally mature person who ever walked this earth! Jesus was confident yet humble, assertive yet not pushy. When He reproved people for their sin, it was always for their welfare and benefit. He modeled forgiveness.

[22] Knowing God has forgiven us can motivate us to become more forgiving. Whenever we feel like evening the score with someone, we need to think about Jesus' example. We gain increased freedom as we learn how to deal with all the baggage we've been carrying around. He wants you to enjoy perfect fellowship with Him. He wants to be able to guide your life so that you have a purpose in all that you do. He wants you to know and experience love, joy, and peace. Even though it is impossible to live without sinning (I John 1:8) we should always strive to please God. And if we fail, we can go to Him and confess our sins.

[23] We've learned how sin was brought into the world. God's love has been demonstrated throughout Scripture through His relationship with mankind. His ultimate act of love was send-

---

21-22 How can we be like Jesus?

23 Where did "love" originate?

ing His only begotten Son. Is it any wonder that God created humans for fellowship? Love is an act enjoyed by every human being on earth. We are born with a craving to love and be loved — where did love originate if not with Almighty God?

Hopefully you have now become a child of God so your place in the new heaven and new earth is reserved (Revelation 21:27). Read the next chapter and find out what happens when you die.

What happens when I die, do I go straight to heaven or do I sleep in the grave? What about those who reject Jesus as their Lord and Savior – where will they go? There are some people who believe we cease to exist after death – is that true?

CHAPTER 4

What Happens When You Die?

This is a subject that many people would rather avoid. They reason, "I have a neighbor down the street who is a drunk and dishonest man... I'm better than he is... I don't really do bad things, so surely nothing bad will happen to me after death." This is human reasoning, but it doesn't fit in God's plan. There are some absolutes in our world even though many choose not to recognize them. Life and death are absolutes — you are absolutely alive or absolutely dead — then what? It is up to you and me to decide now which path we choose in the next life — life everlasting with God, or eternal destruction. God is a loving God and He wants the best for us!

We have a spirit

[2] He (God) formed the spirit within man (Zachariah 12:1). It is with our spirit that we identify with God for He is Spirit; (Romans 8:16) therefore, we worship Him in spirit and truth (John 4:24). Man bears God's spiritual image (Genesis 1:26, 27) so that he can know God in a personal way but he is still God's creature (Job 14:14, 15). Our spiritual image is the non-material part of mankind. The image would include major elements:

reason, conscience, and will;
a rational moral free agent;
attributes belonging to his own nature as a spirit;
capable of communion/relationship with his Maker.

---

1 Are there absolutes in our world?
2 In what ways are we made in the image of God?

Mankind's design is distinguished from all other inhabitants of this world, and raised immeasurably above them. He belongs to the same order of being as God Himself, making him superior to beasts and animals.

At death the spirit leaves the body

[3] Your spirit body is clothed with flesh and when you die your spirit leaves the body (Ecclesiastes 12:7). The apostle Paul looked forward to being with Christ at death (Philippians 1:21-24; 2 Corinthians 5:1-8; 2 Peter 1:13, 14). While we're in our physical bodies, we cannot see God, (I Timothy 6:16) but in a new, spiritual body, fitted for life in a spiritual realm, the faithful will live in His presence (Revelation 22:4).

Old Testament Saints

[4] Those in the Old Testament who died in God's favor were spoken of as "being gathered to their fathers" (Genesis 25:8,17; 35:29, 49:29, 33). They were buried in Canaan, but Moses was buried in Moab and no one knew where his grave was (Numbers 27:12,13; Deuteronomy 34:5,6). The gathering place was called "sheol" in the Old Testament and "hades" in the New Testament. God is God of the spirits of all mankind (Hebrews 12:9; 12:23; Mathew 22:31, 32). When our spirit leaves the body, the body is dead (James 2:26).

Dr. Dave Reagan explains it this way:

[5] The Bible indicates that after the death of Jesus on the Cross, He descended into Hades to declare the good news that He had shed His blood for the sins of Mankind (1 Peter 3:18-19 and 4:6). The Bible also indicates that after His resurrection, when He ascended into Heaven, Jesus took

---

3 What happens when we die?

4 Where did the O.T. saints go at death?

5 What did Jesus do right after His death? When did the O.T. saints go to heaven?

Paradise with Him, transferring the spirits of dead saints from Hades to Heaven (Ephesians 4:8-9 and 2 Corinthians 12:1-4). The spirits of dead saints are thereafter pictured as being in Heaven before the throne of God (See Revelation 6:9 and 7:9). The spirits of the righteous dead could not go directly to Heaven before the Cross because their sins were not forgiven. Instead, their sins were merely covered by their faith. The forgiveness of their sins had to await the shedding of the blood of the Messiah (Leviticus 17:11; Romans 5:8-9, and Hebrews 9:22).

Events at Death

[6] So, what happens when you die? If you are a child of God, your spirit is immediately ushered into the bosom of Jesus by His holy angels. Your spirit remains in Heaven, in the presence of God, until the time of the Rapture. When Jesus comes for His Church, He brings your spirit with Him, resurrects and glorifies your body, making it eternal in nature (1 Corinthians 15 and 1 Thessalonians 4). You reign with Jesus for a thousand years and then live eternally with Him on the new earth (Revelation 20-22).

Preparing for Eternity

[7] One thing is certain: *"Every knee shall bow and every tongue confess that 'Jesus is Lord!'"* (Isaiah 45:23 and Romans 14:11). Your eternal destiny will be determined by when you make this confession. If it is made before you die, then you will spend eternity with God. If not, then you will make the confession at the Great White Throne judgment before you are cast into Hell. To spend eternity with God, your confession of Jesus as Lord must be made now. *"If you confess*

---

6   If you are a child of God, what will happen when you die?

7   What will your eternal destiny depend on?

with your mouth Jesus as Lord, and believe in your heart that God raised Him from the dead, you shall be saved." (Romans 10:9) —www.lamblion.com

A Person's Eternal life is out of Reach of other People

[8] How much harm can people do to us? They can inflict pain, suffering, and physical death. But not a single person can rob us of our future beyond this life. How much harm can we do to ourselves? The worst thing we can do is to reject God and lose our eternal future with Him. (John 3:18). Man can kill our body, but he can't destroy our soul or spirit (Matthew 10:28). Life placed under God's protection is safe. God places his own seal, the Holy Spirit (Ephesians 1:13) on his followers, guaranteeing his protection over their soul (or spirit). Our physical body may be beaten, maimed, or even destroyed, but nothing can harm our spirit when we have been sealed by God.

Those who reject Christ

[9] People who reject Christ are refusing God's offer of eternal life in a perfect world. They are identifying with the enemy of God, Satan. There's nothing that would please Satan more than have us reject Jesus Christ. Satan was called Lucifer before rebelling against God (Genesis 3:1-17;Isaiah 14:9-15; Ezekiel 28:13-15; 2 Corinthians 11:14). There will be a judgment day, as explained by Dr. Reagan:

The Certainty of Judgment — By Dr. David Reagan

[10] The apostle Paul emphasized the certainty of judgment. In Romans 2:16 he wrote, *"God will judge the secrets of men through Christ Jesus."* And in Romans 14:10, 12 he stated, *"We shall all stand before the judgment seat of God...*

---

8 What is the worst thing that can happen to us?

9 How do we please Satan?

10 Will each one of us be judged?

So then each one of us shall give account of himself to God." The writer to the Hebrews summed it up succinctly: *"It is appointed for men to die once and after this comes judgment"* (Hebrews 9:27).

[11] This comes as a surprise to most Christians. Some find it hard to believe. I'll never forget when I realized it from my study of Scripture. I became filled with so much joy that I felt like jumping pews all day!

[12] Let me put it to you in another way. If you are truly born again, then you will never stand before the Lord and be judged of your sins. That's because the judgment for your sins took place at the Cross.

[13] You see, all your sins, and mine, were placed upon Jesus as He hung upon the Cross, and the wrath we deserve was poured out upon Him (2 Corinthians 5:21). He became our substitute. He took our judgment for sin (Romans 8:3 and Galatians 3:13).

[14] If you have appropriated the blood of Jesus to your life by accepting Him as your Lord and Savior, then your sins have been forgiven. They have also been forgotten in the sense that God will never remember them against you again (Isaiah 43:25 and Hebrews 8:12). Think of it — forgiven and forgotten! That is grace! —www.lamblion.com

Hell

[15] If we are to avoid hell, we need to be on guard against the work of Satan the devil (I Peter 5:8). He is the accuser of the brothers (Revelation 12:10). It is his desire that we follow him instead of the Almighty God. If we allow Satan to have his way by rejecting the grace and mercy God has provided through Jesus Christ (Matthew 25:46) and continue until death, we will face

---

11-14 Why will believers never be judged for our sins?

15-16 Why is it important to make good choices?

the consequences (Daniel 12:1,2; Acts 24:15; Revelation 20:11-15). Hell is described in the Scriptures as a place of darkness and sadness (Matthew 22:13), a place of fire (Matthew 5:22), a place of torment (Revelation 14: 10), a place of destruction (Matthew 7:13), and a place of disgrace and everlasting contempt (Daniel 12:2). **For details on the view of hell see: http://www.lamblion.com/articles/articles_issues5.php**

[16] Life is all about making choices. Each and every day we make decisions. Some are good and some are bad. There are always consequences. The most important decision we make in life is our choice to obey God to the best of our ability each and every day. In order to do this, we need to *know* God — read the next chapter and find out who God *really* is.

What can a person know and understand about our Creator God? What does it mean, "God in three persons?"

CHAPTER 5

Knowing God
The Father, Son and Holy Spirit

Who is God the Father?

God is the One and only true God who has revealed Himself as Father, Son and Holy Spirit. He is all knowing, all powerful, and everywhere present at the same time. He is from everlasting to everlasting (Psalm 90:2), the self-existent Creator of the universe. He is the architect and originator of life and blessedness. He is called the LORD Almighty, Redeemer, the first and the last (Isaiah 44:6-8, 24). His Being, His character, and His will are the themes that all the biblical writers endeavor to explore. His character is revealed in Scripture over and over. As we learn more about the character of God, we can better understand His:

> expectations,
> > justice,
> > > warnings,
> > > > judgments, and
> > > > > promises for obedient mankind.

Many Old Testament saints are mentioned in Hebrews 11 as heroes of the faith. Much has been recorded about their adventures and relationships with God. We'll take a look at just a few of these mighty men of old and their walk with Him. Take note of how they knew and trusted God.

---

1 What does Scripture say about God?

Noah

[2] Picture God telling you He is going to bring floodwaters that will destroy a corrupt generation! Would you believe Him? Noah did and as a result, he and his family along with every animal species were spared. Until this time, it had never rained. How could anyone believe the earth would be covered with water! God was pleased with Noah's obedience (Genesis 7:1-4) and made a covenant with him (Genesis 9:12, 17).

Abraham

[3] Imagine how you would feel if you were told to leave your country! This is what happened to Abraham. God promised that he and all the families on earth would be blessed through him (Genesis 12:1-4) and Abraham obeyed God. Abraham had a continuing relationship with God. When God saw the horrible sin that was taking place in Sodom and Gomorrah, He said He would destroy them. Abraham pleaded with God, thinking surely there were some righteous people there. Conversation actually took place between God and Abraham concerning what God was about to do. God said He would not destroy the cities if Abraham could find ten righteous people there. Talk about a close relationship — they had one! (Genesis 18:16-33). God made a covenant with Abraham (Genesis 17:7) and promised that his descendants would be blessed because of his obedience (Genesis 22:16,17).

Jacob

[4] Abraham's grandson, Jacob, also obeyed God and God gave the same Abrahamic covenant to him and made the same promise (Genesis 35:9-12; 46:2-4; 48:3,4). Jacob's name was changed

---

2 What took place between God and Noah?

3 What took place between God and Abraham?

4 What was Jacob's name changed to and what was significant about it?

to Israel. This was the beginning of the nation of Israel as a people (while they were still wandering in the dessert). Later they settled into the state called Israel (Exodus 6:8); however, the boundaries extended much further then than they do today (Joshua 1:2-6).

Moses

⁵ Can you imagine, while going along and tending to your own business, you suddenly come upon a bush that is burning, and yet isn't consumed? That happened to Moses. And as if that wasn't shocking enough, a voice was heard calling his name, "Moses, Moses." He was told to take off his sandals because he was standing on holy ground! (Exodus 3:2-5). After God explained His purpose for calling Moses, He revealed His name to him, distinguishing Himself from all other gods (Exodus 3:13-15; 6:2-8).* Moses was called to lead the nation of Israel to the land God had promised to Abraham and his descendants.

David

⁶ The book of Psalms contains countless events that display the relationship between David and God. David prayed for God to keep him as the apple of His eye (Psalm 17:8) and God considered him to be a man after His own heart (I Samuel 13:14). God promises an everlasting kingdom through the offspring of David (2 Samuel 7:8-13). The New Testament is the historical record of God keeping His covenant made with Abraham, through the linage of David in the person of Jesus. God is continuing to keep His covenant with Israel and the Gentiles yet today. This is made possible through God's son Jesus. Isaiah prophesied His coming, *"...prepare the way for the LORD (God); make straight in the desert a highway for our God"* (Isaiah 40:1-3). Who was this person?

---

5 Who did God say He was? *(see appendix D)

6 What did God promise through David?

Who is the Son, Jesus?

[7] After reading the scripture above, if you had been John the Baptist, do you think you would have known that Scripture was speaking of *you*? John knew, because he understood the book of Isaiah. Can you imagine how John felt when Jesus came to be baptized? There he stood baptizing people in the Jordan river saying, *"Repent, for the kingdom of heaven is near"* (Matthew 3:1-3), and then Jesus showed up! John was the "voice calling in the desert," saying, *"Prepare the way of the Lord (Jesus), make his paths straight."* Jesus, God in the flesh had arrived on the scene! (John 1:1-3, 14).

[8] Jesus came to glorify the Father (John 17:1,4) and as He revealed His identity to His disciples, they came to understand who He *really* was! He was the I AM! Now when He told this to the Jews, why do you think they picked up stones to throw at Him? (John 8:57- 59). The Jews who were questioning him recognized the name, "I AM." They knew Jesus was expressing His oneness with the Father. They knew Scripture and were familiar with Exodus 3:14. They recognized the name, "I AM," in the Old Testament as the name of their One and only Creator God. That's why they wanted to stone Jesus for claiming to be God. Jesus told the Jews the importance of believing who He claimed to be (John 8:23, 24). Following are just a few of the apostles who understood who Jesus *really* was.

Paul recognized Jesus as the:

King (Lord) of Glory
(I Corinthians 2:8-10; Psalm 24:7-10),

"fullness of God" – the totality of God
(Colossians 1:19),

---

7 How does Isaiah 40:1-3 compare with John 1:1-3?

8 Who did Jesus claim He was?
   Who was Jesus according to Paul, John, Peter and Thomas? (˙Appendix E; ˙˙F)

firstborn over all creation
(Colossians 1:15-19; Psalm 2:6-8).*

John recognized Jesus as:

God (John 1:1-3, 14),**

No other god was formed before Him
(Isaiah 43:10),

The first and last
(Revelation 1:7, 8, 17, 18; Isaiah 44:6).

Peter knew Jesus as "our God and Savior"
(2 Peter 1:1-2), and answered the most important
question ever asked (Matthew 16:13-16).

Thomas knew Jesus as his Lord and God
(John 20:28,29).

Who is the Holy Spirit?

[9] It's truly great for a Christian to know the Father and the Son, but there's a special excitement in knowing the Holy Spirit (John 14:16-18), because He empowers us.

- Jesus said the Holy Spirit would be our Teacher, Comforter, and Revealer of Truth (John 14:25, 26; 16:13-15; Luke 12:11,12). We are told not to lie to the Holy Spirit (Acts 5:3,4) – notice verse 4 says, "lied to God."
- The Holy Spirit spoke to and sent the disciples (Acts 20:22,23; 13:2,4; 10:19,20)
- We can depend on the Holy Spirit to intercede for us (Romans 8:26, 27).

---

9 How does the Holy Spirit work in our lives?

The fullness of God is expressed in 2 Corinthians 13:14, *"The grace of the Lord Jesus Christ, and the love of God, and the fellowship of the Holy Spirit be with you all."* Take note of how the Holy Spirit works in our lives explained by Dr. Reagan:

The Baptism of the Spirit - by Dave Reagan

[10] So, let's take a look at Holy Spirit baptism. I believe there are at least three types of Spirit baptism. The first is what I call the baptism of the Holy Spirit. I think it occurs at the point of conversion.

[11] The Bible teaches that the Holy Spirit is God's Evangelist, drawing unbelievers to Jesus (John 16:7-11). But when a person accepts the testimony of the Spirit regarding Jesus, the Spirit ceases to operate externally. That's because the Spirit takes up residence inside the believer (1 Corinthians 3:16). The Spirit becomes Jesus' "birthday present" to the new, born again child of God.

[12] When the Spirit moves in, He regenerates the person's dead spirit (Acts 2: 38), seals the person for redemption (Ephesians 1:13-14), and gives the person at least one spiritual gift (1 Corinthians 12:7).

The Baptism *in* the Spirit

[13] The second type of Holy Spirit baptism is what I call the baptism in the Holy Spirit. This is what I think Paul had in mind when he said, *"Be filled with the Spirit"* (Ephesians 5:18). It is also what I think Jesus had in mind when He said that He wants us to be so full of the Spirit that the Spirit will flow out of us *"like a river of living water"* (John 7:37-39).

[14] To be baptized in the Spirit is to be immersed in the Spirit to the point that the Spirit takes over control of your

---

10-12 How is the baptism "of the Spirit" explained?

13-15 Explain the baptism "in the Spirit."

life — of your thoughts, words and actions. You see, it is one thing to have the Spirit residing in you. It is another thing to have the Spirit presiding in you. Likewise, the Spirit can be a resident in you without being the president in you.

¹⁵ Many Christians have quenched and grieved the Spirit within them because they have treated Him as an unwanted guest. This is due to the fact that many Christians have accepted Jesus as Savior but not as Lord.

The Meaning *of* "Spirit-filled"

¹⁶ To be baptized in the Spirit is to be filled with the Spirit. Although this baptism in the Spirit can occur at conversion, it usually happens at a later time. It is a result of learning how to walk with the Lord in obedience to His will.

¹⁷ This baptism can be a gradual experience, occurring over a long period of time, as a person slowly yields more and more of his life to the Lord. It can also be a very sudden experience, resulting from a major crisis that drives a person to his knees in total surrender to the Lord.

¹⁸ It can also be an experience that occurs more than once. The point is that we are all leaky vessels. We can get full of the Spirit, and then through neglect of our spiritual life, we can drift away from the Lord and begin once again to quench and grieve the Spirit.

¹⁹ Repentance will then bring us back to the Lord and to a new release of the power of His Spirit within us. Thus, we experience again the baptism in the Spirit. The only way we can stay full of the Spirit is to stay near the fountain, Jesus Christ (Hebrews 12:1-2).

16-19   What is the meaning of "Spirit-filled?"

The Baptism *by* the Spirit

[20] The third type of Spirit baptism is what I call the baptism by the Holy Spirit. It is the special anointing that God gives a person to empower him or her for service in the kingdom.

[21] Jesus received such an anointing at His water baptism (Matthew 3:13-17). The Apostles received this anointing on the Day of Pentecost (Acts 2). Paul received this special anointing at a prayer meeting in Antioch (Acts 13:1-4), sixteen years after his conversion on the road to Damascus.

[22] This is the anointing I pray for every time I get up to preach. It is the anointing I prayed for when I began writing this article. It is the anointing every person should pray for when they get ready to do any work in the Lord's kingdom, whether it is to preach, teach, sing in a choir, or serve as an officer of the church.

The Sign of Being Spirit-filled

[23] …The greatest evidence of a Spirit-filled life is not a particular gift of the Spirit. It is the fruit of the Spirit: *"love, joy, peace, patience, kindness, goodness, faithfulness, gentleness and self-control"* (Galatians 5:22-23).

A Plea for Restoration

[24] The Church began with a great outpouring of God's Spirit (Acts 2). The Bible says that the Church Age* will conclude with another great outpouring of the Spirit (Joel 2:28-29). I believe we are in the midst of that "latter rain" right now.

[25] We need to open ourselves up to the movement of God's Spirit. We need to release the power of the Spirit in our individual and corporate lives. We need to restore the Holy

---

20-22 Explain baptism "by the Spirit."

23 What are the signs of being Spirit-filled?

24-25 When did the outpouring of God's Spirit begin? What should we do now? (*Appendix G)

Spirit to His vital role as God's Energizer in all our efforts to expand the kingdom. —www.lamblion.com

Father, Son and Holy Spirit

[26] Most have difficulty understanding how God reveals Himself in three distinct personalities. God the Father, God the Son (Jesus) and God the Holy Spirit are of the same substance. Our finite mind cannot fully comprehend how this can be, but think of the ocean and its beauty, how vast it is, the calming sound of the waves as they come to shore. You would like to share this magnificent ocean with your friends but they can't come to see it, so you do the next best thing. You fill a jar of ocean and send it to your friends. They can't begin to understand how that jar of water could be ocean — they can taste it and feel it — but that's the closest they can get to know what the magnificent ocean is like. Think of the ocean as being God — but much greater because He is in the entire universe at the same time — He's all knowledge — all knowing and all powerful. He wants to come to the earth, but we can't look at Him and live, for His glory would be too magnificent for us to bare. So He "dips out of Himself" (a jar of water/ocean) and sends His son (Word/God) to the womb of Mary. At birth, Jesus was fully God and fully man (water/ocean). And if you drink the (water/ocean) you have the Holy Spirit inside of you (Jesus is called, "living water."). [This may be a very poor analogy in trying to explain how such a wonderful God could share Himself with His own creation!] How can our finite minds begin to comprehend Him? There you have a minute picture of the three distinct personalities, God in three persons. Jesus came to show us the Father (John 14:9). He came from the Father (like the jar of water from the ocean).

---

26 What is one way to explain God in three persons?

[27] Just as a jar of ocean (water) was sent to a friend to show what the ocean was like, God sent His son Jesus, as a man, to show us the Father and glorify Him (John 17:1-4). He was fully God and fully man without mixture. Jesus limited Himself to our environment as a human being in order to communicate with us. Jesus said:

I AM the Bread of Life (John 6:35, 41,51)
  I AM the light of the world (John 8:12; 9:5)
    I AM the gate for the sheep (John 10:7,9)
      I AM the Good Shepherd (John 10:11,14)
        I AM the resurrection and the life (John 11:25)
          I AM the way, the truth and the life (John 14:6)
            I AM the true vine (John 15:1,5).

Jesus is:

The first and last (Revelation 1:17)
  The Redeemer (Galatians 3:13)
    The Image of God (Colossians 1:15)
      Mediator between God and man (I Timothy 2:5)
        The Mighty God (Isaiah 9:6)
          Name above every name (Philippians 2:9)

He is the Son of God who obeyed His Father perfectly, humbling Himself by being born as a human being and coming to earth to die for the sins of the world. He gave up the heights of heaven for the depths of death.

[28] All efforts to explain Almighty God fall short because of our human frailties in trying to describe Him. An illustration's short-coming has to do with the limitations of human language and our finite minds. He is the One who holds the world in

---

27 Who did Jesus say He was?

28 How can seeking God benefit us?

balance. We can't begin to comprehend His greatness! But just from what we read about Him in the Bible, we get a glimpse of a righteous, Holy God. How awesome it is to experience His love, peace and joy in our lives and observe it in the lives of others (I John 4:7).

You too, can know God personally and have a relationship with Him. You can be in covenant relationship with Him (Jeremiah 31:33; Luke 22:20). Would you seek Him as you would silver and gold? (Proverbs 2:1-5; Mathew 7:7). If so, you will draw close to Him (James 4:8). Jesus said He will never forsake you (Hebrews 13:5). Read the next chapter and learn how you can know God personally and walk in His way.

I can see how people in the Bible knew God — they had a personal relationship with Him, but can I really do that?

CHAPTER 6

Your Personal Relationship
with God

Yes, of course you can. God desires for each and every one of us to love Him with our whole heart, soul and mind. This is the beginning of your relationship with Him (Mark 12:30; Proverbs 8:17). Relationships are ongoing. That's how we *remain* in Christ (John 15:1-10). God desires our obedience and things always go better when we do things His way. He has our best interest at heart.

God speaks to us through the Bible, our instruction book (Proverbs 2:1-5; Matthew 7:7). This is how we understand what is expected of us (Proverbs 1:2-7; 4:5). By reading the first four gospels we learn what Jesus taught about honesty, integrity, fairness, justice, rewards and punishment as well as many other things that will help develop character. And, of course, by reading the teachings of the apostles, we learn more about life principles. By reading 1 Corinthians 13 we learn that love is the greatest gift. When we humble ourselves before God, it will improve our relationship with Him (I Peter 5:6-7). God cares for us (I John 3:21,22; 5:14,15). Good relationships are always better when we communicate on a regular basis. We need to talk to Him every day just like we talk to our friends. And we need to listen (Psalm 46:10; I John 3:21-22). The Bible is God's written word and by reading it daily, we listen to Him daily. Although

---

1 How can we have a personal relationship with God?

we become Christians instantly by faith in Christ, we develop a stronger personal relationship with Him as we learn the Scriptures. There are no short cuts to maturity.

Loving God

[2] The more you come to know the Lord, the more you will love Him (I John 4:8). And the more you love Him, the more you will desire to be with Him. We always desire to be with those whom we love. You will experience a walk with the Lord that transcends anything possible in this life. We were created for fellowship with God (I John 1:3,4) and that purpose will reach its zenith in the eternal state as we live in God's presence. There may be days when you can only pray and read God's Word for a few minutes at a time, but set aside as much time as possible.

The following article will show you how to talk to God and pray effectively. It is written by David Welsh, senior minister at Central Christian Church in Wichita, Kansas. The A.C.T.S. model is used by many and David has adapted it this way:

Prayer — A.C.T.S.
(Adoration, Confession, Thanksgiving, Supplication)

[3] Begin prayer with worship. It sets the tone for the entire prayer. It reminds us whom we are addressing, whose presence we have entered, whose attention we have gained. This way, we don't focus prayer like a wish list, but instead we commit ourselves to the Almighty God. We need to slow down and focus on Him.

[4] We can praise God for being faithful, righteous, just, merciful, gracious, willing to provide, attentive, and unchanging. When we spend a few minutes praising God for

---

2   What will strengthen our love for God?

3-4   How can we forget about ourselves during prayer?

who He is, we forget about ourselves and concentrate on the greatness of God.

How to Adore God

[5] When facing major decisions, we may concentrate on His guidance. When suffering of inadequacy or guilt, we may praise Him for His mercy. When in need, we may worship Him for His providence or power.

[6] Pick out a psalm of praise and read or say it to Him. Some of the best known are Psalms 8, 19, 23, 100 and 148. Go through the whole book and see what you can find. Why not sing a song of praise! This may be awkward at first, but like anything else new in our life, it can be learned if we are disciplined. Why not stretch yourself?

Confession: A Neglected Art

[7] Often we hear people pray publicly, "Lord, forgive us for our many sins." In our private prayer time, instead of throwing all our sins onto a pile without so much as looking at them, why not name them, one by one, and confess them. When we deal with sin specifically, we would say, "I told so-and-so there were nine hundred cars in the parking lot when really there were only six hundred." That was a lie, and therefore I am a liar. I plead for your forgiveness for being a liar."

[8] Or instead of admitting I had been less than the best husband, I would say, "Today I willfully determined to be self-centered, uncaring and insensitive. Please forgive me for that."

Benefits of Confession

[9] First, your conscience will be cleansed. "I finally said it,"

5-6 How can we adore God?

7-8 Give an example of how we can confess our sin.

you will think. "I'm finally getting honest with God, I'm not playing games anymore and it feels good." Next, you will be flooded with relief that God has a forgiving nature. Knowing that *"as far as the east is from the west, so far has he removed our transgressions from us"* (Psalms 103:12), you will begin to learn the meaning of peace.

[10] Then, you will feel free to pray, "Please give me your strength to forsake that sin from here on out." With the power of the Holy Spirit, you can make a commitment to give up the sin and live for Christ. And that's when your life begins to show signs of change.

[11] As God goes to work on your sins, you begin to see Paul's words being fulfilled in your life: *"If anyone is in Christ, he is a new creation; the old has gone, the new has come!"* (2 Corinthians 5:17).

Expressing Thanks

[12] Psalm 103:2 says, *"Praise the Lord, O my soul, and forget not all his benefits."* Paul writes in I Thessalonians 5:18, *"Give thanks in all circumstances, for this is God's will for you in Christ Jesus."*

[13] There is a difference between feeling grateful and expressing thanks. The classic teaching on this is in Luke 17:11-19, the story of the ten men healed of leprosy. How many of those men do you think felt tremendous gratitude as they walked away from Jesus, completely healed of their incurable, disgusting, socially isolating disease? There's no question about it — all ten did. But how many came back, threw themselves at Jesus' feet and thanked him? Just one.

[14] In this story we catch a glimpse of Jesus' emotions. He is moved: first to disappointment by people, who felt gratitude

---

9-11   What things will help us work on sin in our lives?

12-14   What is the difference between being grateful and thankful?

but didn't take the time to express it, second to satisfaction by the one who came all the way back to say thanks. We need to thank God every day for four kinds of blessings: answered prayers, spiritual blessings, relational blessings and material blessings.

Asking for Help

[15] But then it's time for supplications – requests. Philippians 4:6 says, *"In everything, by prayer and petition, with thanksgiving, present your requests to God."* If you have adored Him, confessed your sins and thanked Him for all His good gifts, you're ready to tell Him what you need.

[16] Nothing is too big for God to handle or too small for Him to be interested in. We can say, "Lord, I don't know if I have the right to ask for this. I don't know how I should pray about it. But I lift it to you, and if you'll tell me how to pray, I'll pray your way."

[17] God honors that kind of prayer. James says, *"If any of you lacks wisdom, he should ask God, who gives generously to all without finding fault, and it will be given to him."* (James 1:5).

[18] Other times, we may say, "God, this is my heart on the matter, and I'd really like you to do this. But if you have other plans, far be it from me to get in the way. You've asked me to make my requests known, and that's what I'm doing. But if what I'm asking for isn't a good gift, if the time isn't right, if I'm not ready to receive it, no problem. Your ways are higher than my ways, and your thoughts than my thoughts. If you have different plans, I'll go your way."

[19] We need to pray for the ministries we're in touch with. For the church we attend, for their leadership and for the

---

15-17 How can we be honest with God in prayer?

18-19 What is a good attitude when making requests?

congregation. For the people we're involved with. For those who don't know God – that He will draw them to Himself.

[20] For family, and other loved ones. We need to ask Him for help with decisions about finances, education, vacation time, jobs, etc.

[21] We need to pray for our character. "God, I want to be more righteous. Whatever you have to bring into my life to chip away at my character, bring it on. I want to be conformed to the image of Christ."

[22] Break up your requests into whatever categories suit your purposes, and then keep a list of what you've prayed about. After about three weeks, go back and reread your list. Find out what God has already done. In many cases, you will be amazed.

[23] I've found the ACTS formula especially helpful when I write out my prayers. Starting with adoration, I might write something like this: "Good morning, Lord! I feel free to praise you today, and I'm choosing this moment when I'm fresh and ready, willing and able to get going, to stop and say that I love you. You are a wonderful God. Your personality and character bring me to my knees. You are holy, just, righteous, gracious, merciful, fair, tender, loving, fatherly and forgiving. I'm thrilled to be in a relationship with you today, and I worship you now."

[24] After adoration I move to confession. I might write: "Please forgive me for committing the sin of partiality. It is so much easier for me to direct my love and attention toward those who seem to 'have it all together.' Without even realizing it, I find myself avoiding troubled people. I'm sorry. Thanks for your impartiality to me. Please forgive me, and now I claim your forgiveness." Then I take my pen

---

20-22 Why is it good to pray for our character?

23 Give an example of adoration.

24 Give an example of confession.

and cross out what I've written, saying, "I thank you that I'm free from this. I'm glad the slate is clean. Thank you for forgiving me."

²⁵ The thanksgiving is easy for me. I thank God for specific answers to prayer, for helping me in my work, for people's responsiveness, for protecting our elders and staff and board, for material and relational blessings and for anything else that makes me particularly happy. Thanking the Lord for every day keeps me from being covetous, and putting my thanks on paper reminds me of the incredible number of blessings I enjoy.

²⁶ I'm glad that supplication is last. Once I've worshiped God, confessed my sins, and given thanks, its okay for me to take out my shopping list. In fact, James 4:2 says, *"You do not have, because you do not ask God."* I used to be vague about what I needed. "Please help me and cover me and keep me out of trouble." I don't do that anymore. I list specific requests, leave them with God and regularly review them to see how He has answered them.

²⁷ When I get up from praying, I feel as if a ton of bricks has been lifted off my shoulders. I Peter 5:7 says, *"Cast all your anxiety on him because he cares for you."* When I pray, I'm not just telling God my problems, I'm turning my biggest concerns over to Him. Once I've put them in His capable hands, I can go about my day in His strength, free from crushing concerns. Practice these steps and see what God does in your life!

Notice Colossians l 1:9-14 – prayer is life changing. Ask God to fill you with the knowledge of His will through spiritual wisdom and understanding. Pray this in order that you may live

---

25 Give an example of thanksgiving.

26 Give an example of supplication.

27 What is a good way to start our day?

the life worthy of Jesus' name – baring fruit, making your life count, through good works and joyously thanking the Father. The Holy Spirit will nudge you in developing your character, that of being – trustworthy, respectful, responsible, truthful, kind and honest.

A Godly relationship produces Christian Maturity

[28] Prayer and Bible reading are stepping stones toward maturity. Just as a baby should not stay on milk and needs solid food, a Christian needs to leave elementary things and press on toward maturity (Hebrews 5:11-14). Maturity is measured not only by our living example, but how we develop good relationships with people. When we are getting along well with our loved ones, we feel secure. Imagine how much more security we have when we have a good relationship with God (2 Corinthians 6:16; Jeremiah 31:33). As we mature in our relationship with Christ, we begin to move from elementary principles to considering how God will use us in this life. We begin to mature when we look at the spiritual gifts that God makes available to us.

Notice what Dr. Reagan has to say about our spiritual gifts:

The Significance of Spiritual Gifts (by Dave Reagan)

[29] Paul says in 1 Corinthians 12 that every person who is born again receives at least one supernatural spiritual gift from the Holy Spirit. A person may receive more than one gift. And, if you are a good steward of the gifts you receive, then you may receive additional gifts as you develop spiritually (Luke 19:26).

[30] God expects us to use our spiritual gifts to advance His kingdom. This is what the judgment of works will be all about. Each of us who are redeemed will stand before the

---

28 What is a sign of maturity?

29 According to Paul, how many gifts do we have?

Lord Jesus and give an accounting of how we used our gifts to advance the kingdom of God on earth.

[31] We will be judged as to the quantity of our works (Luke 19:11-27; Romans 2:6-7). We will be judged as to the quality of our works (1 Corinthians 3:10-14). Finally, we will be judged as to the motivation of our works (1 Corinthians 4:5).

[32] There will be degrees of rewards. They will be manifested in the crowns we receive (2 Timothy 4:7-8), the robes we wear (Revelation 19:8), and the degrees of ruling authority which we exercise with the Lord (Luke 19:11-27).
—www.lamblion.com

God's warning

[33] If the fruit of the Spirit is present in our lives, relationships will go well (Galatians 5:22-24), but if we're walking in the flesh the opposite is true (Galatians 5:19-21). When we sin we feel guilty, when we repent, we are forgiven. We should strive to live a good life. By doing so, we will be much happier. If we are living the life that God expects, we will avoid evil thoughts from coming into our heart – we need to guard our heart. Thirteen sins that Jesus said come from the heart are found in Mark 7:20-23:

> evil thoughts,
> > adulteries,
> > > fornications,
> > > > murders,
> > > > > thefts,
> > > > > > covetousness,
> > > > > > > wickedness,
> > > > > > > > deceit,

30-32 What does God expect of us and how are we judged?

33 What makes a happy life?

lewdness,
    an evil eye,
        blasphemy,
            pride, and
                foolishness.

[34] If we claim to be a Christian and live a disobedient life, we become hypocrites (Matthew 15:7-9). The devil is content to let us profess Christianity as long as we do not practice it. He goes about like a roaring lion (I Peter 5:8). We can avoid pitfalls by seeking God's counsel in every area of our lives (Matthew 6:33; Luke 11:9-12). When we're tempted we should seek the Lord for help (James 1:12-16; Philippians 4:13). Your phone line to God is prayer. You are talking to the Almighty God of the universe, the Holy One Who created you and knows your inward thoughts. His unfailing love is always there for you! You can praise Him for:

Who He is and for the gift of salvation,
    His glory (worth/value), marvelous deeds, greatness,
        Creation, strength, majesty, holiness,
            Sovereignty, judgments, justice, righteousness,
                and truth.

God's purpose for your life

[35] God has a plan for each of us (Jeremiah 29:11). What things do you feel you need to change in your life in order to have a good relationship with Christ? Remember that His call is primarily a spiritual one, which involves a re-evaluation and shifting of priorities in your life. There are many people around you who need Jesus Christ, especially your own family. Jesus

---

34 How can we avoid failure?

35 How do we know God will help us?

died for everyone - the famous, the rich, the poor, the alcoholics, drug addicts, and those who have lost their way in life. He loves the person who is out of work, the person who is caught in the web of adultery, the lonely teenager, and the one frustrated with business. He loves you. And if you let Him, He will not only direct your path, but will give you power to live according to His purpose (2 Timothy 3:17). This does not mean you'll never have any suffering and trouble in your life. But you are promised that if you lean on the Lord in faith, He will walk through the suffering with you and supply all your needs. The prophet Isaiah expressed it this way and we are promised:

> " *When you pass through the waters, I will be with you*
> *and through the rivers they will not over flow you.*
> *When you walk through the fire,*
> *You shall not be burned,*
> *nor shall the flame scorch you.*
> *for I am the LORD your God,*
> *The Holy One of Israel, your Savior.. "*
> (Isaiah 43:2-3)

36 Our God is a "God of hope." Put your hope and trust in Him. He will sustain you through any crisis that may come your way.

> *"The steadfast of mind,*
> *Thou will keep in perfect peace,*
> *because he trusts in Thee.*
> *Trust in the Lord forever,*
> *for in God the Lord,*
> *we have an everlasting Rock"*
> (Isaiah 26:3-4 NAS).

_____

36 What hope does Isaiah give?

Recognizing your personal relationship with God

[37] As you grow in intimacy with Jesus, you'll learn to recognize God's voice, which makes it easier for you to understand His will for your life. It will not be an audible voice, but he speaks to the heart, and it will always agree with the Bible. We are able to more easily accept His perspective and Godly advice about the important issues of life such as family matters, financial decisions and commitments that could otherwise distract you from His will. Who but our Lord would give us a specific purpose and then arrange it so that our pursuit of it would lead us to carrying out His will in all areas of life? What a stress reliever!

[38] As you seek His will and His guidance by reading His Word and praying, remember – Satan is there to turn you away. Read the next chapter and learn about the danger of taking the wrong path.

37-38   What is the acid test of knowing we hear from God?

JESUS

ATHEISM

ADVERSARY

HERESIES

DRUGS

What would the wrong path look like? How can I avoid it?

CHAPTER 7

Beware of Taking
the Wrong Path!
Destructive Heresies – False Teaching

Once you've accepted Jesus Christ as your Lord and Savior and have made a decision to follow Him — Satan will always be around with a desire to devour you (I Peter 5:8; John 8:44). He will continually attempt to entice you many different ways. It could be well meaning people who want to convert you to their false religion. They want you to take the path they've chosen. It can be so deceptive that it's difficult to discern the difference between truth and error. Since Jesus and the apostles warned about dangerous heresies, Christians need to always be on guard.

[2] Satan loves to imitate everything God does. He wants to be our god, after all he is the god of this world (2 Corinthians 4:4). His desire is for us to follow him. There are many false religious groups who call themselves Christians — in fact most of them will emphatically claim they are the only true religion. Their followers don't realize they are being deceptive because they themselves are deceived. This has always been the case since the days of the apostles and continues today throughout the world. What better way can Satan deceive others than by making Jesus a lesser person than who He really is? False teachers (2 Corinthians 11:13-15) masquerading as the one and only true religion will teach a "different Jesus." They will deny He was God in the flesh. We'll take a look at how Paul addressed this issue in his day.

---

1 Why does the Bible warn us about deception?

2 According to 2 Corinthians, how does Satan disguise himself?

The Apostle Paul's Warning

[3] The apostle Paul told the early Christians that just as Eve was deceived by the serpent's cunning, they were being led astray from their sincere and pure devotion to Christ. He was concerned about their taking the wrong path, and warned them, "If someone comes to you and preaches a Jesus other than the Jesus we preached, or if you receive a different spirit from the one you received, or a different gospel from the one you accepted, you put up with it easily enough." (2 Corinthians 11:4)   (In other words, they were putting up with a false teaching, when they shouldn't). Isn't it wonderful that the Almighty God cares for us so much that He has given instruction on just about every matter that comes up in life?! Oh, if we could only listen to God's Word, we could avoid so many pitfalls in our lives!!!

The Gnostics Taught a "Different Jesus"

[4] The Gnostic teachers imitated the apostles in the way they took the gospel from place to place. It was customary for believers to take the missionaries in as they came to teach them in their homes, and they gave them provisions for their journey when they left. So when the Gnostic* teachers also called on these believers, the apostle John addressed the situation of providing food and lodging. In 2 John (7-11) he was writing to urge discernment in supporting traveling teachers; otherwise, someone might unintentionally contribute to heresy rather than truth. The Gnostics were teaching a "different Jesus." They refused to accept the truth of the incarnation because they did not believe you could mix the holiness of God with flesh. They took this position because they considered all material things to be inherently evil. They therefore taught that Jesus was a spirit being

---

3 What warning does Paul give?

4 What was the different gospel the Gnostics taught and how did John address it? (*Appendix H)

— an angel who was neither fully God nor man. In doing this they denied both the physical death of Jesus and His bodily resurrection. This is the reason that John told the early Christians to test all teachers by asking them to confess "that Jesus Christ has come in the flesh" (1 John 4:2).

Could You Be Misled by a Knock On Your Door?

⁵What if you were a new Christian and you were so excited about your new life in Christ and eager to learn more, and some very loving and kind person knocks on your door and leaves you an interesting piece of literature that seems very biblical. Perhaps you read it and believed it was biblically correct, so when they came back and offered you a free home Bible study, you were ready and willing to learn from them. You can save a lot of time and heartache by first addressing their belief concerning the question that Jesus asked, "Who do you say I am?" If their teaching is different from what you learned in chapter 5, a red flag should go up. For example, if they explain that Jesus is an angel named Michael, and that he was God's first creation in heaven, you know they have a different Jesus. They may tell you that Michael was just one of many names given to Jesus. They may not tell you the truth in the beginning – that they believe Jesus (Michael the archangel) was God's first creation. Once the personage of Jesus is diminished, then men or an organization can replace Him by saying in effect, "Come to *me* for salvation."

⁶They might also redefine the personage of the Holy Spirit, by saying He is just a mere active force. This is a "different spirit." If they tell you that only "they" (the ones who write their literature) have the Truth, and that you must identify and do works with them in order to have eternal life, you know they have a

---

5-6 What is the acid test of a false gospel?

different gospel. And to make matters even worse, if you joined them, your life could be controlled to the extent that should you leave the group and identify with another church, you could be expelled and all members including family would have nothing to do with you again.

Could You Be Misled by a TV Ad?

[7]Sometimes during an ordinary TV program an ad will appear offering a free King James Bible. Now, what could be wrong with that? In fact, someone delivers it to your door, and they too, offer to come in and teach you their leader's interpretation of the Bible. They too, are loving, kind people who are very sincere about their beliefs. They are also good moral people. In fact they do some wonderful things like have family time every week. But do they have a different Jesus? It's important to always address the same question, "Who do you say Jesus is?" (Matthew 16:15,16). Sometimes their answers can be so obscure that it's difficult to discern the error because they have been taught to be deceptive, even though they don't realize it, and that's because they're deceived too! They might tell you that Jesus Christ is the first baby born to God in heaven and is the Brother of Lucifer, the devil - one of several gods created by the super god, Adam, an exalted man. They may say that God the Father is a resurrected human man who is a married being who has "spirit children" in heaven. They might explain that every human being born on this earth was first born in the pre-existence to God the Father and one of his wives in heaven, just like all other human and demonic beings. They too will try to convince you that they are the only ones in the world who have the Truth! There are hundreds of groups claiming to be Christian but are teaching false doctrine.

---

7 What is another way we should be on guard?

Things to look for

[8] Some groups have published their own Bible, claiming they've corrected all the mistakes made in other translations. You can identify groups who have a different gospel by taking note of the following things:

- They redefine who Jesus is and deny the true One;
- To the Bible is added the authority of their own publications;
- A False Basis of Salvation — they add to the finished work of Christ, works;
- Uncertain Hope — they never have the assurance of salvation;
- Presumptuous Messianic Leadership — they claim that they represent God;
- Teaching — they change their views;
- The Claim of "Special Discoveries" — they alone have the Truth.

[9] Groups claiming to be the only true Christians will often choose a verse here and there that seemingly supports their view. In doing so, contextual setting is ignored. They also seek to dominate the total life of their followers. Some ask for huge sums of money in order that they might live lives of luxury. Often they denounce others — blacklisting all other churches and denominations. Some innocent people will say, "But they're so good and kind, how can they not be true Christians?" Remember, Satan appears as an angel of light (Galatians 1:8.9).

A Serious Matter

[10] This is a very serious matter because our salvation depends upon our relationship with Jesus, the one true God who

---

8-9 How can you identify someone who is teaching a different gospel?

10-11 What is the one most important thing we need to be right about?

revealed Himself to the world by becoming incarnate in the person of Jesus (God in the flesh). There is salvation in no other person (Acts 4:10-12). There is salvation in no other way (John 14:6).

[11] We can be wrong about many things, but if we are right about Jesus, we can be saved. Likewise, we can be right about many things, but if we are wrong about Jesus, we can be lost. To be saved, we must put our faith in Jesus, the Jesus revealed by the Word of God (John 17:3).

[12] There's a problem in far too many churches today where destructive doctrines have influence them. Their false teachings (1 Timothy 4:1) are creeping into the mainline church in many forms. It is not at all unusual anymore to hear some denominational leaders deny the divinity of Jesus or His bodily resurrection or His second coming. One of the favorite themes today is the teaching that there are many different roads to God — that God has revealed Himself in Buddha, Confucius, Abraham, Jesus, Mohammed, and many other persons. The natural conclusion of such thought is that it is improper for Christians to seek to convert people from other religions to Jesus. If this were true, Jesus died for nothing!

[13] Another danger that exists is a resurgence of spiritism in our world today. This belief says that the dead can be contacted and can communicate with the living. Unfortunately, there are those who consult mediums in every major city in the United States today. It's a sad state of affairs when demon deception convinces people that their loved ones have been contacted.

[14] And worse yet is Satanism. In some areas, Satan himself is worshiped. A Church of Satan operates in San Francisco, and the "church of Antichrist" has several branches. The Names of some popular rock groups and the words of many of their

---

12   How has false teaching influenced some churches?

13-14   What are some other concerns we need to be made aware of?

songs reflect their satanic influence. We should avoid them like the plague!

A Challenge

[15] The Word of God challenges us to test everything because we are all subject to deception. We are to prove all things (I Thessalonians 5:21). We are exhorted to test ourselves, as well. Here's how Paul puts it: *"Test yourselves to see if you are in the faith; examine yourselves!"* (2 Corinthians 13:5). The test of all teaching and all doctrine is the Word itself. We are called to be like the Bereans who tested everything Paul taught by the Word of God (Acts 17:10-11).

[16] Will you be able to discern truth from error? Can you defend your faith? (Jude 3). Keep in mind the true gospel (I Corinthians 15:1-5).

Finding the Right Church

[17] First, seek God's wisdom in finding the place where He desires for you to learn, fellowship and serve. Second, read their statement of faith, making sure they hold to orthodox teaching:

God created everything that exists,
  The Bible is the only infallible authority,
    Unique deity of Jesus and Virgin Birth,
      Trinity – Tri-unity of God,
        Bodily resurrection of Christ,
          Universality of Sin,
            Salvation by grace alone,
              Bodily return of Christ,
                Eternal punishment of the unredeemed.

15-16 What is our challenge?

17 What things should be noted in a statement of faith?

[18] You do not want to identify with a church that is too legalistic or cultish. Dr. Reagan lists five ways in which some churches can be cultish:

A Church can be Orthodox in its Doctrines and yet be "Cultish" in its Practice:

1. Am I dominated by a church leader? (A good leader will guide their students to think for themselves and rely on the Bible as their lives are transformed).

2. Am I asked questions relating to my personal life that go beyond biblical principles? (A spirit-led leader will trust people to do right, unless they have reason to think otherwise).

3. Am I made to feel like I'm constantly being "observed" as though someone is ready to correct me of wrong doing? (A good leader will not insist that people follow the leader's own personal convictions that go beyond biblical principles).

4. Am I taught that I belong to the only true church and all other denominations are in error? (A good leader will only stress the essential biblical doctrines, and extend liberty in nonessentials.

5. Am I taught that I am "free in Christ" in making my own plans for my life, or am I taught "how" to plan my life according to the dictates of a church leader? (A good leader will encourage people to seek God's will for their lives, through Bible Study, prayer, and a Bible based church).

18 Name some cultish practices in some churches.

**Recommended reading: Churches That Abuse by Enroth.
—www.lamblion.com**

Read the next chapter and learn how Christians should view the world and how they can live in it and yet not be a part of it.

How should I view the world and what are my Christian responsibilities?

CHAPTER 8

The World View and YOU

Every time we read the newspapers and watch the news on TV, it's evident that we're living in frightening times. We have:

> radical groups who want to destroy us,
>> unfriendly countries developing nuclear bombs,
>>> people dying from dreaded diseases,
>>>> violence of all kinds,
>>>>> illegal immigration,
>>>>>> polygamy out of control,
>>>>>>> an economy that has taken a nose dive, and
>>>>>>> foreclosures on many homes.

[2] Moral values are declining and corruption in this country is greater than ever before. Many families are no longer connected and far too many children are out of control. Atheism is on the rise. People are wondering what the next generation will be like.

[3] And as if all of this is not bad enough, our own U.S. Department of Homeland Security web site has implied that a number of large respected church denominations are potential terrorists. These denominations hold most of the same views as did the founders of our U.S. government! This is unbelievable considering how our schools, hospitals, and orphanages were all founded by the same like-minded people of faith. In fact, the Bible was used as a text book in our schools where children learned to

---

1   What is the evidence of our troubled times?

2-3   What is troublesome in our own government regarding our historical values?

memorize Scripture, and they recited the Lord's Prayer as part of the curriculum.

[4] An atheist who opposed prayer in school used her son as an example to take prayer out of school. Later that son became a Christian and has shared his testimony all over the world.

[5] For the first time in America's history, we have cell groups right here on our own soil training people to kill us. These groups believe Americans are infidels. They also believe they are pleasing their god by killing us. Yes, we're living in the time when evil is called good, and good, evil (Isaiah 5:20).

A Changing Culture

[6] Our culture is changing rapidly, and it's having an effect in every area of our society. Now, what about you? Where will you stand on vital issues of today? Unfortunately, some of these views have been made into a political issue. The sanctity of life has been challenged! Take abortion for example. Until a few years ago abortion was considered to be an evil offense against the unborn child, and there was a law against it – now that has changed. As a result, more babies have been left to die right after birth than ever known before, and some found in the garbage. If you've had an abortion, and you now believe it's wrong, remember that God is a loving and forgiving God.

[7] Until recent years, pornography was never seen on television programs and movies. Much of our crime is attributed to this. Never before in America have so many little girls and boys been abducted and had horrible things done to them. If you've ever been involved in such things and now consider it is wrong, remember that God is a loving and forgiving God.

[8] In times past marriage was considered a sacred union — "until death do us part" — and now too many marry with the

---

4-5 What sort of evil things are going on that some call, "good"?

6 How has the attitude of abortion changed?

7-8 What other things have changed drastically?

intention of leaving, if all does not go well. Marriage was always between a man and a woman, and now this is changing also (Romans 1:26,27; I Corinthians 6:9-11). People are living together not married and this no longer shocks people; in fact, it's accepted. If you've ever been involved in such things, remember that God is a loving and forgiving God.

The World
[9] The world would have you believe that all of these things are normal, that we should all be tolerant, but God does not tolerate these things (Ephesians 5:5). It seems the world is consumed with sex. There is nothing wrong with sex within the confines of marriage. The fact is, God designed sex to be a beautiful gift. Some think God and the Bible are against sex. That's not true. He created it and wants us to enjoy it. Marriage, and sex within marriage, should never be looked down upon. God Himself said, *"Marriage should be honored by all, and the bed undefiled; but fornicators and adulterers God will judge"* (Hebrews 13:4). Talk to anyone whose parent was having an affair while they, as children, were growing up, and you'll discover one of the reasons God hates adultery. It devastates children. Talk to any girl whose boyfriend got her pregnant, and then left her, and you'll be reminded why God hates sexual immorality (I Corinthians 6:13-18). If you've engaged in any of these things and have repented, remember that God is a loving and forgiving God. God loves you and wants to transform your life (Romans 12:2). He loves us the way we are, but He loves us too much to leave us that way!

Drugs
[10] Until recent years, the only drugs ever heard of were prescriptions drugs, and now they're sold illegally on every corner.

---

9 How does the world's view compare with God's view?

10 What results in taking the wrong drugs?

Our prisons are over-run with abusers and many lives have been destroyed by them. While under the influence of drugs people will rob, rape and murder, doing things they would never have imagined before becoming a user. There are people today who want to legalize marijuana, even though the use of it often leads to hard drugs. Recent polls reveal that many people are trying to cope with stress through diversions like drugs, alcohol, and promiscuous sex. They all lead to immorality, poor health and ultimately unhappiness. If you've been involve with drugs and now realize they're wrong for you, remember that God is a loving and forgiving God and He knows what is best for you.

[11] God gave laws and commandments for a reason. His instructions work for the good of all mankind. When we are obedient, life will go better. We may go astray from time to time, but if we ask for forgiveness and turn back to God, He will forgive us. We are secure in God's unfailing love regardless of how many times we fail Him. If you lean on Him, He will guide you each day of your life. You may be overcome at times with all kinds of troubles and emotions, but He will go through it with you. As you strive to live an obedient life, God's great love will cover you as you learn to trust Him (Psalm 143:8).

Truth

[12] The world would have you believe there's nothing wrong with practicing the things mentioned above. They may also believe that no one person has the right to make a judgment concerning another's spiritual beliefs. They say, "You have your truth and I have mine – or what you believe is right for you – and what I believe is right for me. Have they not created their

---

11 How can we get help?

12 Who is the real Truth?

own god? This could be a disaster eventually with all kinds of gods making all sorts of rules! Christianity, on the other hand has been demonstrated for two thousand years and it works because it is THE TRUTH – and that's because Jesus is the TRUTH (John 14:6). Even if no one ever applied a single Christian principle to their lives, the Christian faith would stand true because of what God has done in history through the finished work of Christ on the cross.

[13] Truth is not like clay that each person can mold as he or she wants. Truth is like the law of gravity. I may believe I can fly when I jump off a tall building, but my different view of the truth of gravity won't change my landing speed. Truth doesn't change, even if the majority of people believe otherwise or it becomes politically incorrect. Facts are always true. So it's very important that we learn the facts and the truth about Jesus. God's word is truth (John 17:17). *"He who trusts in himself is a fool."* (Proverbs 28:26). We're always safe trusting in Jesus and the biblical view – let's consider it now by Dr. Reagan:

Jesus' Viewpoint by Dr. David Reagan

[14] The crucial point for you to consider is the biblical view. Let's look at it, and as we do so, compare the biblical view with your own. Let's begin with the viewpoint that Jesus told us we should have. It is recorded in John 12:25 — *"He who loves his life loses it; and he who hates his life in this world shall keep it to life eternal."*

[15] Those are strong words. They are the kind that causes us to wince and think, "Surely He didn't mean what He said." But the context indicates that Jesus meant exactly what He said. So, what about it? Do you hate your life in this world or do you love it?

---

13   Why should we not put trust in ourselves?

14-15   How does John compare loving our life with that of the world?

The Viewpoint of the Apostles

[16] The apostle Paul gave a very strong warning about getting comfortable with the world. In Romans 12:2 he wrote: *"Do not be conformed to this world, but be transformed by the renewing of your mind."* How do you measure up to this exhortation?

[17] Are you conformed to the world? Have you adopted the world's way of dress? What about the world's way of speech or the world's love of money? Are your goals the goals of the world — power, success, fame, and riches?

[18] The brother of Jesus expressed the matter in very pointed language. He said, *"Do you not know that friendship with the world is hostility toward God? Therefore, whoever wishes to be a friend of the world makes himself an enemy of God"* (James 4:4).

[19] Are you a friend of the world? Are you comfortable with what the world has to offer in music, movies, television programs and best selling books? Friendship with the world is hostility toward God!

[20] In fact, James puts it even stronger than that, for at the beginning of the passage I previously quoted (James 4:4), he says that those who are friendly with the world are spiritual adulterers.

[21] The apostle John makes the same point just as strongly in 1 John 2:15-16: *"Do not love the world, nor the things in the world. If anyone loves the world, the love of the Father is not in him. For all that is in the world, the lust of the flesh, and the lust of the eyes, and the boastful pride of life, is not from the Father, but is from the world."*

[22] There is no way to escape the sobering reality of these words. Do you love the world? If so, the love of the Father is not in you!

16-17   How do we reflect the ways of the world in our lives?

18-20   How does James address the issue of being a friend of the world?

21-22   How does John address the issue of being a friend of the world?

The Focus of Your Mind

23 Paul tells us how to guard against becoming comfortable with the world. In Colossians 3:2 he says, "Set your mind on the things above, not on the things that are on earth." In Philippians 4:8 he expresses the same admonition in these words: *"Finally, brethren, whatever is true, whatever is honorable, whatever is right, whatever is pure, whatever is lovely, whatever is of good repute, if there is any excellence and if anything worthy of praise, let your mind dwell on these things."*

24 As these verses indicate, one of the keys to living a triumphant life in Christ — to living a joyous and victorious life in the midst of a world wallowing in despair — is to live with a conscious eternal perspective.

25 I have personally found this to be so important that I carry a reminder of it in my shirt pocket at all times. It is a small card that was sent to me in 1988 by the great prophetic preacher, Leonard Ravenhill. The card says, "Lord, keep me eternity conscious."

26 What does that mean? In the words of Peter, that means living as *"aliens and strangers"* in this world (1 Peter 2:11). Similarly, in the words of the writer of Hebrews, it means living as *"strangers and exiles"* on this earth (Hebrews 11: 13). Paul put it this way: *"Do not set your minds on earthly things, for our citizenship is in heaven"* (Philippians 3:19-20).

27 The great Christian writer, C.S. Lewis, explained that to live with an eternal perspective means "living as commandos operating behind the enemy lines, preparing the way for the coming of the Commander-in-Chief."

28 Are you focused on this world? Are you attached to it, or do you have a sense of the fact that you are only passing through, heading for an eternal home? —**www.lamblion.com**

23-24   How can we guard against becoming like the world?

25-28   How can we view our time here on planet earth?

Your **Attitude**

[29] There are many people out there who hold to the world view of the day. They're not interested in life after death, they just want what seems right for their life now. If Christians convince them that *God's* way is right, they want to see it demonstrated in the life of a Christian. Does it *really* work?

[30] Christians will be the first to admit that we are never promised that we will not suffer in this life. But we are promised that if we lean on the Lord in faith, He will walk through the suffering with us and supply all our needs (Philippians 4:19). Trials can make life seem not worth living. Focusing on ourselves can lead to despair. But putting our trust in God gives us an entirely different perspective. As long as we live in this world, we can be certain that our all-sufficient God will sustain us. And as His followers, we will always have a divine purpose.

What is your worth?

[31] Self esteem is a great concern throughout our communities. Getting in touch with your inner-self may give some false notion for awhile that you've found yourself, but will this last? You may not be able to depend on yourself in times of crisis. Everything may be great today in your life, but then you get a phone call:

> that a person dear to you has been killed in an accident,
>> someone took their life,
>>> someone has betrayed you,
>>>> you lost your savings, your job, or
>>>>> you only have two months to live.

[32] Perhaps you've tried to stop bad habits and just can't seem to live a life worth while. You can't count on your inner-self in

---

29-30   Who should we focus on when going through trials?

31   Can we always rely on ourselves in times of crisis?

times like these, but Christians believe the Lord is present with them no matter what each day brings. It may be a day of:

joy or sadness,
sickness or health,
success or failure.

No matter what happens to them today, they believe the Lord is walking beside them,

strengthening them,
loving them,
filling them with faith, hope and love.

[33] As He envelops them with quiet serenity and security, their foes, fears, afflictions, and doubts begin to recede. As Christians, we believe we can bear up in any setting and circumstance because we know the Lord is at hand, just as He told Paul in Acts 18:10, *"I am with you."*

[34] Practice God's presence, stopping in the midst of your busy day to say to yourself, "The Lord is here." And pray that you will see Him who is invisible – and see Him everywhere. *"Seek the* LORD *while He may be found, call upon Him while He is near"* (Isaiah 55:6).

Encouragement

[35] What an encouragement to live for Him! Our strength for the present and hope for the future are not based on the stability of our own perseverance but on God. No matter what our need, we can count on the Father's faithfulness.

[36] If you've been living a life of sin, make a decision to ask for forgiveness and ask God to help you clear the slate and start over. Change takes time! You need to change those things that

32-34 How can we practice God's presence?

35-36 Is it possible to really make changes?

are not acceptable before God. Feelings of insecurity will begin
to fade as you allow yourself to be taught by the Holy Spirit
(John 14:26). Through the indwelling power of the Holy Spirit
we have the strength to overcome the world and walk faithfully
with the Lord (I John 4:4).

[37] Look for opportunities and ways you can change your life.
Don't blame others — that will never help and don't depend on
others to make things work. You'll feel better when you decide to
live your own life well. If you can't forgive yourself for mistakes
in your life, you are rejecting what Christ did on the cross. If you
have a dark past, the blood of Christ can make you well. Lift
your head and walk forward — others and especially children
will model your self esteem. Practice talking to God all through
the day, asking him to take negative thoughts and replace them
with good thoughts. Learn from your mistakes and ask God to
increase your faith. Count all your blessings and be grateful for
what you have — this will kill worry.

Help

[38] Invite someone to walk by your side. Ask a strong Christian
to be your prayer partner, someone with whom you are willing
to open your heart, in order to grow in love. Loving relationships
are packed with tears and laughter, and they can stimulate new
attitudes and action. Ask God to take you from where you are
today to where he wants you to be.

[39] Relationships are not always loveable – in fact they can
sometimes be ugly. But we are to pray about them and our enemies as well (Luke 23:34). If we're holding a grudge against
anyone, we need to forgive them (Mathew 6:13-15).

[40] Remember that warm feelings and emotional enjoyment are
not the goals of love. Love is caring about God's eternal relation-

---

37   How can we make changes work?

38-40   How can you get help?

ship with others. Pray to God that you will see the best in the lives of those you find troublesome or difficult. We all love those "good feelings" that some seek through drugs but as TV preacher, John Hagee says, "There's no "high" like the Most High!" Read the next chapter and find out about the church and you.

Do I really need to attend church?
I'd have a lot more time if I didn't go!

CHAPTER 9

The Church and You

Becoming a Christian is an individual decision. Living out the Christian life is also a personal matter, but God knows what is best for you and we are instructed to fellowship with other Christians (Hebrews 10:24,25). God provided the Church for singing songs of praise, worship, Bible study and fellowship. The Greek word translated church means called-out ones. The origin and beginning of the church are recorded in the Gospels, and the development of it is recorded in Acts. In each community, as a group of believers gathered, a church was formed. These churches were diverse in racial and social backgrounds, but they had certain common beliefs and objectives which united them in spirit with their brothers and sisters in other places. They were convinced that Jesus Christ was God's Son, and had come to give them life. They were committed to sharing this message with the whole world.

²Paul compared the church to the human body, with its many functions and relationships. Every part is honored, every part is needed to work effectively (Romans 12:4-8; I Corinthians 12:14-27). Members met together at appointed times, usually on the first day of the week. They met to worship God, to share with each other, and to partake of the Lord's Supper in remembrance of the death of their Savior (Mark 14:22-24). They parted from each other in order to share with others the good news of Christ. They often met in secret because of persecution. They had a deep love for one another and were even willing to give up

---

1 What does Hebrews 10:25 tell us about fellowship?

2 How is the church compared to the human body?

personal possessions for the good of the body. Study the first few chapters of Acts for a clearer understanding of the church.

Church is not Perfect

[3] There are many people outside the church who hold the world view of today. But secretly they are searching for a moral anchor — they have a hole in their heart that needs to be filled with God. Usually people like this are resistant to rules and they don't like to be told what to do, but they are generally open to reasoning. They wonder if Christianity works and they look for wisdom in others. They want to see a lifestyle that truly reflects biblical values. This is why it's important to find a good Bible believing church.

[4] Some churches in the New Testament had considerable difficulty. The Corinthian church experienced a number of serious problems which Paul sought to correct through his letters to them. Churches today experience similar difficulties. There aren't any perfect churches just as there are no perfect people. If you found a perfect church it wouldn't be perfect when you arrived! (Romans 3:10). Some have said, "I don't go to church because there are hypocrites there." Yet, they go to the grocery — do you suppose there are no hypocrites there? The church serves as a sanctuary, a place of safety, a place where you can find friends who will understand you. It's a place for all people with all sorts of problems and difficulties in their lives. In other words, it's like a hospital for people who need a healing for their soul. It's a place for a continual study of the Word of God. It's a place where Jesus prayed we would all be one (John 17:22). Regardless of your background, the church is the place to receive mercy. Jesus came to save sinners. Paul said he was one of the worst (I Timothy 1:15; 1 Corinthians 15:9). Imagine God saving a person who

---

3-4 How can attending church be beneficial?

had been killing His people! Yes, that's the kind of God we have — no matter how many times we mess up, He has mercy on us. He can mold us like clay (Jeremiah 18:6). The church is a place where friends can help us if we stray and go down the wrong path. We're supposed to speak truth in love to one another.

Bible Study

[5]Getting involved with a Bible study group can be very beneficial to your life. There are classes for every age group beginning with the nursery. The Bible is taught in a very interesting way for the children on their age level; however, parents should not leave all Bible instruction up to the church. The youth pastor not only teaches the Bible, but encourages the youth to become engaged in activities that reach out to their community. Most churches have a class for singles and sometimes they meet the person they eventually marry.

[6]There's another advantage in studying the Bible with a small group — they become good friends/family to you. This is a place where you can share your heart and ask people to pray for you, and you can pray for others. And of course, there's always food! Here you can find people who are sensitive and responsible to the social, moral and spiritual needs in the community.

[7]Often groups go on missionary trips in foreign lands where they learn about other cultures and teach Bible classes. There are many people who went to church as babies and have grown old with their church friends. This kind of Bible study and fellowship is important to God and he made it all possible through the church.

The Purpose of the Church

[8]The purpose of the church is to enable Christians to gather

5-7 How can studying the Bible with others help?

8 What is the mark of Christianity?

to help each other in their spiritual journey, and to carry out the commission of Christ to make disciples in every nation and teach these disciples to follow Him (Matthew 28:19,20). This would be following the commandment given by Jesus to love one another (John 13:34). We can love others even if we don't agree with them. We're to love others unconditionally. We are not only to love one another but we're told to love our enemies also (Mathew 5:44). Love is the trade mark of Christianity. Our love from Christ is our source. There are many people that are dying for this kind of love. Serving the church financially and physically will bring blessings to your life. You can discover how God will use your spiritual gifts and how you can use them among your fellow Christians (I Corinthians 12:1-12)

[9] God still calls men and women to be His ambassadors today. He challenges us to serve Him — sometimes close to home, sometimes in distant lands. The question for us is, "How will we respond to His call?" May God give us the courage to say, *"Here am I! Send Me"* (Isaiah 6:8). Often we do not feel qualified, but according to (2 Timothy 3:16,17), we will be equipped for every good work.

Your Part

[10] If you have found this book to be helpful, would you be willing to read it with someone? It's a quick and easy way to make new relationships and spread Truth with others. *"Go therefore and make disciples of all the nations, baptizing them in the name of the Father and of the Son and of the Holy Spirit"* (Mathew 28:19).

[11] We know that Jesus is coming again (Luke 21:27; John 14:3). We have no idea when it will be, but we do know we are living in times that are critical. None of us know how many days

---

9 How should we respond to our faith in God?

10-11 What is the only thing we can take to heaven?

we have on this earth. If you thought you only had a short time left, what do you think would be the most important thing to do? We can't take riches, and treasures with us to heaven, but we can take people. If you knew your neighbor's house was on fire, would you not try to save them? Do we care about people whether they are lost or not? Do we care about them dying and going to hell? If we have love for others, why not reach out to them with the love of God.

[12] Our hope and dream is that each person who reads this book will share it with one other person, and if at all possible read it with them. We need to spend time, face to face with others. We need to do our best to reach the community. What would happen if every Christian would reach out to one other person? The Bible is the answer for our sick and dying world.

Reaching the Heart

[13] What makes people do crazy things? Why did executives of large corporations walk away with billions of dollars that affected the whole world? The answer is, *"There's a huge problem with the heart"* (Jeremiah 17:9). Their hearts were greedy! The result of their greed caused a domino effect from the top down, reaching into the pocket book of the poorest man on the totem pole. When people sin they hurt many others. Matthew 15:18 says, *"For out of the heart proceed evil thoughts, murders, adulteries, fornications, thefts, false witness, blasphemies."* These are the things that defile people. How can the heart of mankind be reached? The Bible says that the word of God knows the intent of the heart (Hebrews 4:12) and is sharper than any two-edged sword. By applying our heart to understanding and seeking God's wisdom (Proverbs 2:2-4) we can have a pure heart (I Timothy 1:5; Hebrews 10:22).

---

12 What is the most loving thing a Christian can do?

13 What is the root cause of our problems?

[14] The heart is mentioned in hundreds of verses throughout the Bible. Only God knows and understands the deep emotions of our heart (I Samuel 16:7). How can you know if your heart is right with God? Ask God to search it (Psalm 139:23,24). When we examine ourselves God will reveal all sorts of baggage hanging on us like a yoke. We are like a boat with barnacles which need to be scraped off. As we allow God's pure love to seep into our heart, the barnacles of hate, hurts and unforgivness will gradually disappear. We harbor wounds through hurts and life experiences. The consequence of sin in our lives – whether it is a result of something we deliberately did or whether it's a result of another person's action, we are like broken fences that need mending. Often, we know we're forgiven by God for our sins, but we choose to remember them - we're like a leaky roof, or cluttered room that needs to be cleaned out. That's the way we are! Who else but God can fix such problems? Doctors and pills can do their work, but they can't fix the most intricate part of our soul – only God can do that! Once again, the answer is found in the Bible, *"You shall love the LORD God with all your heart, with all your soul, and with all your mind"* (Matthew 22:37). Loving God will not only bring peace and comfort but you will have a happy heart that makes the face cheerful (Proverbs 15:13). Meeting with small groups studying the Bible can be very beneficial in understanding the heart problem.

Our Nation has Changed

[15] Our nation was founded on the Bible. For 200 years it has been the leading nation of the world — the super power. We had churches on every corner that were full. People loved and cared for one another. We had character, integrity, honesty, and the majority of people believed in the orthodox teachings of the

---

14 How can hearts be changed?

15 What was America like in the past?

Bible. They put them into practice. People were conscientious. America was truly America the beautiful. But we now see our nation on a slippery slope. So if we ask, "What can I do," why not do your part by helping to mend the soul of another person. Encourage them to go to God's word, attend church and fellowship with Christians.

[16] Perhaps you can recommend this book to your evangelism team in your church. The congregation could give names of people whom they would like to receive a visit — each one could teach one! Serving starts with presenting ourselves to God, *"I beseech you therefore, brethren, by the mercies of God, that you present your bodies a living sacrifice, holy, acceptable to God, which is your reasonable service"* (Romans 12:1). Our responsibility is to serve God faithfully, wherever He has placed us. Then we leave the results to Him. As Jesus reminded His disciples in John 15:5, *"... Without Me you can do nothing."* May the Lord bless you as you do your part in helping to spread the Word of God.

Read the next chapter and find out how God has transformed the lives of people from many different walks of life!

---

16 How are we to serve God?

Transformed Lives

◆ **Larry Locke's Testimony**
From drugs and despair to an ordained minister

I was raised in the Roman Catholic religion but was never religious. I attended Catholic school most of my formative years, served as an altar boy, learned the catechism and went regularly to confession but I did not know God as I know him now.

I was raised in a home where perfection was expected [yet never exampled] and a home that smelled of alcohol and fear each and every day. I longed to escape and live life on my own. Little did I know that living on my own as a teenager would be much more frightening. Because I lived in an oppressive family environment it became easy for me to develop my new found freedom without boundaries. As a teenager, and on into my early 20's, I believed that I was free to do anything. I experimented with PCP [more commonly known as "angel dust" or "speed"], heavy drinking, gambling on NFL football games and the ponies, shooting pool for money, stealing [the grand larceny kind], fighting and the like. My involvement in these vices expanded into dealing drugs and because of this enterprise I carried with me a Smith and Wesson 357 Magnum, Browning 9mm semi-automatic pistol and Nunchuks – all of which I could use very well. It did not take too long for my appetite to exceed my level of income. My life began to spin quickly out of control. My gambling debts, drug needs and "partying" expenses escalated and no amount of stealing, begging money from friends, or successful gambling days could dig me out of my personal Hell. My family and friends abandoned me [and rightfully so], I lost my job - my apartment - and I found myself with very little money in my pocket. I had no where to go and no one to go to – so my home became the streets of Los Angeles. My ritual was to drink coffee at "Denny's" until they closed then find a dark outdoor hallway at some apartment complex to lay my head for the night. It did not take too long before I came to my senses and realized that my life needed to change. Either out of self pity or desperate need – I entered an Air Force recruitment center, enlisted on the spot and signed up to become an air traffic controller.

When I enlisted in the Air Force two things happened – first, discipline entered into my life. Whether I liked it or not I now became accountable for my actions and responsible for my job. The second thing that happened was that the Air Force did not give me the job field that they had promised. Instead I was transferred to a job entitled "radar technician" – the most critical job needed in the Air Force. It did not take long for me to understand why. I worked for NORAD [North American Aerospace Defense Command], was trained in Biloxi, Mississippi and later stationed at an Air Force Installation on an Army Base in Virginia. I worked in a building with dual exterior walls – each eight feet thick – each made of reinforced concrete. My job required me to work 8 hour shifts [at times back to back – at times 8 hrs. on 8 hrs off 8 hrs on…] in a dark room while focusing on an oscillating radar screen. At the time, this job field had the highest rate of alcoholism, drug use, divorce and suicide within any of the Air Force job fields. I could not believe how easy it was to obtain drugs in the military; more easily than when I dealt drugs on the streets of Los Angeles. Twice I found my roommate hanging from the ceiling by his belt when I returned to my dorm.

After my time in Virginia – I came to learn that I was to be stationed for three years at a small remote radar installation in the northern most part of Alaska. I was also told by NCOs who had been stationed there that it was an all male installation and that homosexuality was widespread. It did not take long for me to sink into depression and I too found myself attempting suicide. I was checked into the military hospital, evaluated and diagnosed with severe depression. The military wanted to release me from the Air Force but I told them that I did not want to – I just wanted to work in my promised job field [I had argued for this the entire time I was in the Air Force]. They said that they could not do it – so I was sent packing and given an honorable discharge for medical reasons.

After the Air Force, I moved to York, Pennsylvania. My best friend in the military lived in York and his family took me under their wing and helped me to grow up. I stayed at their home for a while and then branched out on my own – finding my own place to live and started working as a golf professional at a local country club. I also began picking up some college classes at York College and got hooked up with several of their basketball players. One of those players, who was from Johnstown, Pennsylvania, hooked me up with his cousin – a girl by the name of Jamie Johnson; also from Johnstown. Jamie had just graduated from Lancaster General Hospital School of Nursing and was working back in her home town. I proposed to Jamie after 4 months of dating and we were married 6 months later. We settled in the Johnstown area where I attended the University of Pittsburgh at Johnstown. I worked part-time at the university bookstore and with our dual income Jamie and I bought our first house. Life on the outside seemed to settle down – I was in college and doing well, I had a steady job and we had a house. However, my heart and soul was far from settled. My upbringing developed me to be a proud, self-gratifying, highly competitive, violent perfectionist. Not only did I display these traits but I expected many of these from others – including my wife. Our first year of marriage was horrific. We seldom saw eye to eye, we argued and fought constantly, and the smallest thing that she would do or say would send me into a rage. One afternoon, during one of our fights, I lost it. I grabbed Jamie, pinned her to the wall and was prepared to beat her when the image of my father flashed before my mind's eye. Not only had I caused my wife to fear the same fear I experienced in the presence of my father but I had also become very much like the person that I vowed I would never be like. I put Jamie down and left the house – knowing that my marriage was over. I retreated to the golf course – a place I found great comfort during difficult times in my life. It was a rainy and dreary day – no one on the golf course but me – but I played anyway. I played hole number one and two without incident. After teeing off on hole number three I walked off the tee into a deep swale before reaching the fairway. It was in that swale that I looked up to God, who at the time I did not believe in, and said, "If you are real – please help me." Nothing happened – the sun did not start to shine, the birds did not start to sing – as a matter of fact it started raining harder. I thought to myself – What did you expect! After the round I headed home. Jamie and I talked very little that week – she went her way and I went mine – only connecting by sleeping together at the end of the day. A week after our fight, I returned to the same golf course. It was a beautiful sunny day and the course was crowded. The starter paired me with a couple and their son and after teeing off on the first tee we all shared small, casual chit-chat on holes one and two. After we teed off on hole number three and walked into the same swale that I prayed my prayer – the father began to share the gospel of Jesus Christ with me. I was intrigued and listened to him intently. Once the round was over, he came to my home and shared more. He answered all my questions, fielded all my bitterness and frustration with "religion" and calmly talked with me about having a relationship with God. It was there in my kitchen that I accepted Jesus Christ as my Lord and Savior. This man opened up his home to me and my wife, 6 hours a day, 6 days a week for 10 months and mentored me in the faith. It was during this time that I felt the call of God in my life to enter full time ministry – a ministry that I have been actively involved in for 25 years.

◆ Jack Hollingsworth's Testimony
I was homeless and hopeless until Christ came into my life.

Hello, I'm Jack and I hope this little testimony will be of some help to whoever reads it. My life started on a pretty sour note after plans to abort me in the womb didn't happen. I grew up under the care of a mother who resented my existence. Although there were five other kids I never fit in. I always felt like I was on the outside. They were the family. I was just there. My Dad died as a result of an explosion after a gas space heater leaked in the night. Rather than turn on the lights to see when he got up that morning, or maybe he was just lighting a cigarette, he struck a match and opened the bathroom door and the gas exploded. I was four years old when my Dad was buried. I wasn't allowed to go to the funeral because I had gotten dirt on my clothes. An uncle, who was helping out during the time Dad was in the hospital, it turns out, was a pedophile and liked to expose himself to children and try to get them in his bed. My memory about what he did is spotty.

After a time we all moved to north Mississippi where my Mother met a man and after some more time she married him. I had never seen him or met him until she brought him home with her. We had been staying with an aunt. We were wakened in the middle of the night and brought out to meet this man who said he was my daddy now. From that moment my life became a torment. For the next twelve years I was physically and emotionally beaten every day. He beat me with anything he got his hands on from his belt to sticks or water hose, it didn't matter. He was very angry and he was a bully. He beat me in the head with a shoe brush. I still have the scars from living with him. My mother had a vicious tongue. She was constantly reminding me that I was no good and ugly and worthless. She slapped me and hit me but compared to my step-father it was nothing. I would have willingly let her hit me if I could have just felt like I belonged to her. But that never happened.

At fifteen I found the comfort and escape of alcohol when I drank some beer with some buddies. I was so glad I had found something that took the pain and fear away; even if just for a while. At seventeen I nearly killed my step-father when he backed me into a corner and something in me snapped. I blacked out and was brought back when a high school friend who was there started hitting me shouting, Let him go, you're killing him." It was a totally empty victory. I felt worse than ever, it didn't fix anything.

I spent the next twenty-five years chasing that escape and comfort that eventually turned into oblivion. I spent that time in jails, mental hospitals, treatment centers, the streets and abandoned buildings. There were "marriages" that were just desperate attempts to belong somewhere. There was nothing. I attempted to end my life with drugs and once even jumped off the Mississippi River bridge in Memphis, missed the water, landing in the mud and rocks. I couldn't die and I couldn't live.

Sometime in 1986 I ended up in Lexington, KY. There in a detox I met Sally. She was a strange little thing who let me sit in her office at night smoking. She was always nice to me and honest. I was in and out of there for the next three years. She would manage to work in some Bible and the gospel from time to time. On Dec 8, 1988 she told me about Jesus and introduced me to Him and I was born again. I got out of the system and got a real job. After a time the Lord started dealing with me about Sally; said she was going to help me. Then He said she was going to be my help. I knew what that meant so I went to her house one day and told her, "The Lord's been dealing with me and I think He's been dealing with you. Are you ready to get married?" She said, "No, but if you'll give me a minute to change clothes, we'll go."

We have been married for twenty years. With Jesus as Lord and Sally as wife I have found where I fit in. We have been on the road for sixteen years for Acts 29 Ministry. God has been so good to us and used us to lead many to Jesus. We are a faith ministry' never asking for anything. The Lord has opened all the doors. He is our booking agent. I drive and preach and sing. Sally takes care of all the difficult stuff. She coordinates with the home office and schedules everything. We will serve Him until He comes back or calls us Home. MARANATHA!

(Acts29Ministry@aol.com)

◆ Testimonies from a Local Pregnancy Center
April almost aborted her son

The local pregnancy help center is a place where you can fairly quickly find some folks who fit into the category of people whose lives have been transformed by the love of Jesus. Here are two stories that just touch the surface of what we have seen in almost 25 years of ministry.

Jacob and April Munson, were the speakers at our Banquet. Jacob wowed the crowd with his wit and wisdom at the ripe old age of 10 years, and April won every heart in the room with her story of how the Lord took one very confused, broken young woman and turned her life into something truly wonderful. You see, when April came to our pregnancy help center, she was a college student who was estranged from her parents and God because she was spinning out of control in a life of alcohol, drugs and sex. She came to our center, literally on her way to the abortion clinic because a friend of hers begged her to just give us one hour before she went for the abortion. She told us nothing we could say would change her mind, because she had no choice. She was in a bad situation, she was 'not mommy material' and had "already messed this kid up with all the drugs I've put into my body". Our counselor offered her facts about the positive possibilities, a local neo-natal physician came and talked with her, assuring her that if she would quit her drug and alcohol use that day her baby would most likely be very fine. We told her that God loved her and had good plans for her life. That was a turning point for her.

The changes that took place for April were stunning. Satan did not let loose of her easily, but she soon found herself back at church, with her little son, Jacob, who was the glue she needed to pull back into her family. Over the next 8 years, April finished college and went into grad school for her masters in art education. While earning that degree as a single mom, she met Nathan, a master student in opera. They not only fell in love but

Nathan fell in love with little Jacob, who was then 3 years old, and it was a mutual admiration society.

After completing their masters degrees, Nathan asked April and Jacob to marry him. They both said yes! Two days after returning from their honeymoon (just April and Nathan went on that trip), they started legal proceedings for Nathan to legally adopt Jacob. Since then they have had two more beautiful sons, and April is now Doctor April and Nathan is traveling the world singing opera. Jacob is not only a healthy boy, but bright, athletic and loving. This story is no fairytale. Great things happened for April not by waving a magic wand, but by first one then several steps of faith. As God proved Himself faithful to a young, confused and self-destructive young girl, she saw His love and began to trust His heart. Now her heart and her life reflect that same saving grace and love to everyone around her. She and Nathan are raising three young men to be Christ-followers and seeing the affect they already have on every person with whom they come into contact.

Walter's baby was aborted

People don't generally think of men suffering from post-abortion trauma. Actually, most people don't even think about women suffering from it. It is a real and tragic affliction that can have consequences as awful as suicide. Men appear to be better at stuffing the feelings, but we have come to know that they can't be stuffed forever and "Walter" is just one of the many we have come to know and appreciate. He fell into the trap so many have before and since him, of making the mistake of engaging in sex before marriage and when 'caught' by an unplanned pregnancy, chose what looked like the easiest way out - abortion. Today if you ask him about it he answers "Look at me. Do I look like someone who is successful in dealing with my past?" Walter is about 80 pounds over his ideal weight, but more importantly, he is sad to the core of his being. He says that a day never goes by that he doesn't think about that child, wonder what he/

she would have been, what he/she would be doing, how he/she would look, marking every birthday that should have been and every anniversary of that child's death. Not a day goes by in his life that he doesn't regret that decision. The sadness pervades his being.

Walter's victory is in the fact that he gave his life to Christ several years ago, and has accepted the total forgiveness he has because of the atonement of Jesus' death. He is searching for truth in his life and recently discovered that he can turn his tragedy into another person's happy ending by joining a special cadre of men who are training to be male client advocates at the pregnancy help center. "Walter" is now prepared to meet with the young men who come to the center accompanying the young ladies who are considering abortion. He can share how his idea of a 'quick fix' to a problem turned out to be quite the opposite. His loving hand of support will help those young guys not only choose life for their babies, but also lead them into an understanding of a Savior who can take the worst thing in your life and turn it into a ministry. Training for work at the pregnancy help center has not only equipped him to do ministry, but has offered him a program to find the complete healing he needs from his abortion pain. He is excited about being truly free for the first time in over 25 years and knows his life transformation is about to be completed.

Articles submitted by:
Cindy McDaniel - Executive director of Assurance
Women for Life Ministries, Lexington, KY - Phone # 859-278-8469.
www.womenforlife.org - www.assurancereknew.com

◆ Mona Abbott's Testimony
My Healing From Sexual Brokenness and Homosexuality

I want to write a few words of loving encouragement to anyone who struggles with the seductive and tragic stronghold of homosexuality. Also, I want to relate pieces of my testimony about my journey to freedom in Jesus Christ. I used to think that my struggle with same-sex desires was "the one thing that God couldn't touch." How wrong I was! He is the God of the universe and He can bring healing in creative ways we cannot begin to imagine.

I was separated from my birth mother when I was born. She had been the victim of a date rape. Although adopted by the most wonderful and loving parents, I always felt a deep sense of abandonment. I remember one rainy fall day when my third grade class went on a field trip to the Waveland Museum. I recall seeing a fourth grade teacher clutching an umbrella and clinging tightly to one of her female students, shielding her from the rain as they approached a door. I can remember an all-encompassing feeling that came over me. I longed to be held by that teacher with all my heart. Thus began, in innocence and childhood, the roots of a stronghold of sin in my life.

At fourteen, my left breast did not grow. I shunned the boys out of fear of rejection and attached myself more and more to women. I began a cycle of attaching myself to someone who would inevitably reject me and abandon me, a familiar, terrible sort of pain. Sometimes I attached to a friend or teacher. Sometimes I would sink into a fantasy world attaching to a female character on television. For years, I had this horrible secret that nobody knew. My shame was unbearable, but I couldn't stop the cycle. I began to hear about "homosexuals" and thought that surely I couldn't be one of those! But the emotional attachments were beginning to feel sexual.

I began to use drugs to dull the pain. I had a very frightening experience with LSD in 1971, at the age of sixteen. I felt a huge spirit of evil upon me. He taunted me and told me that I belonged to him. He threatened me with annihilation. I began to hope that God would help me. I had always believed there was a God. I didn't know much, but I knew about Jesus in the manger at Christmas. I went to a Baptist Church and when I heard the gospel message, I knew it was Truth. I knew I was sinful and that the only way to have forgiveness was through the cross of Jesus Christ. He was calling me. I "got saved" then and there. Little did I know that the journey to freedom was only just beginning.

In those early days, the churches were not dealing with homosexuality. I was not discipled at my first church. I began to wander in and out of Christian settings. Inevitably the "Sodom and Gomorrah" sermon would come. The truth was preached, without the love. I would be so wounded and broken. I would wander back into the world and take my chances. The brokenness was overwhelming.

I "came out" in 1994. I got involved in the gay community for two years. I met so many women who had been sexually abused as children and abandoned by mothers. They didn't like the stereotyping, but it so often rang true. I found nothing there, only the emptiness of lesbians moving from one relationship to another... more brokenness. And I missed Jesus.

In 1996, after disillusionment with the gay community, I cried out to God. I met Jean Eason that year, and she and Bill adopted me as their "spiritual daughter." While praying one day, the Lord led me to Matthew 6:33, which reads, "But seek first His kingdom and His righteousness; and all these things shall be added to you." I realized that for years I had sought Him, but not first, only second. I had taken Jesus as my Savior, but not my LORD! My emotional neediness had been my God. I had wanted that fulfillment more than anything. That revelation was the beginning of my healing.

Even after His merciful revelation to me, I didn't know how to surrender everything to Him. I was working at a stressful job and soon slipped back into my fantasy world. I had to endure much chastisement before I again fell to my knees. I found a wonderful church with a dear mentor that helped disciple me. Up to that point, I had never acted on my desires.

In 2007, I met a new female friend at church. We both felt God was calling us into ministry together. Then, the unthinkable happened. I became attracted to her. After a few months of the friendship, I confessed my feelings. I fully expected rejection, and even hoped for it, so that we could go on with a platonic friendship. She confessed that she also had feelings for me. You can guess this part. We eventually acted on our feelings. The guilt and shame was terrible. We both went through a period of crying out to God, and He brought forgiveness. As of this writing, we have been friends for two years. So much healing has come from the pain of our initial attraction and sinfulness. The Lord can take evil and make good things come forth. He used my friend's love for me to teach me that I am lovable. From there, I have been able to fully realize how much God Himself loves me. The Lord has shown me what real love for a friend can be. I would never have thought that God could transform what I now see as misplaced and sick love, with true Godly affection. My fantasy world is gone. My emotional longings are gone. Living moment by moment in Him is the greatest joy. He is my lover. Freedom from this stronghold of homosexuality has transformed my mind and heart so much. My past bondage broke me on a daily basis and I can't thank Jesus enough for "binding up the brokenhearted" (Isaiah 61:1). Now, He and I will work on other, less painful, issues!

There are some things I would like to say about homosexuality and gaining freedom from this stronghold. I will use two scriptures: Psalm 37:4 states, "Delight yourself in the LORD; and He will give you the desires of your heart."

This is a promise! If you will truly make the LORD your delight, studying His word, praying and allowing the Holy Spirit to lead you, He will creatively fulfill your heart's desires. If your own desires are sinful, He will replace them with holy desires. Jesus said, "…you shall know the truth and the truth shall make you free" (John 8:32). This is a tough one. The truth is hard to see, and in our flesh, we don't want to see it. (Read Romans 8) This part will be difficult for anyone struggling. I hope any readers will see it as a way to freedom from pain. The truth is actually beautiful and packed with joy! But it may hurt initially.

Homosexual love is not the perfect plan for love that God designed. He made "male and female" to become "one flesh." (Genesis 2:24) No matter how great the longing, same-sex couples can do nothing but try to imitate God's design for intimacy.

People do not choose to be gay. I believe factors in childhood are a huge influence. I know the terrible longing to hear God say that being gay is not a sin. But for me, I could never rest until I found peace with God. Every time, He convicted me. It was sin! I remember when my friend and I were going through our great struggle, trying not to act on our desires and begging God to speak. Was it really a sin…why, why, why? We loved each other! How can love be a sin? I recall reading an Oswald Chambers devotional one day that said that God would never reveal something he had already revealed. There was my answer!

Where does the Bible claim that homosexuality is a sin? There are several Bible verses that deal specifically with homosexuality. (See Leviticus 18:22, Leviticus 20:13, Genesis 19:1-11, Romans 1:26-27, I Corinthians 6:9-10, I Timothy 1:10, Jude 7)

I have read several books published supporting the notion that God condones homosexual love. They attempt to discredit the above verses and validate same-sex behaviors. All I can say is that God has spoken to me and has said, "No." Even more weighty for me is Jesus' sermon on the mount in Matthew 5:27-28. Lust of any type, be it marital, heterosexual or homosexual, involves viewing a creation of God as an object of sexual pleasure. Only the purity of the marriage bed is sacred in God's holy eyes.

The sins of homosexuality involve lust, sexual immorality and most of all, idolatry. Idolatry is *anything* that takes God's rightful place in one's heart. My idolatry was a type of misplaced love. I worshipped the women I was attracted to.

Admitting that homosexual acts and desires are sinful is the first step. Then comes the act of obedience. When my friend and I decided to commit to obedience, God began to pour out blessings. How loving is a God who blesses us for doing what we are supposed to do in the first place! For me, this was the turning point. Isaiah 48: 17-18 states, "I am the LORD your God, who teaches you what is best for you, who directs you in the way you should go. If only you had paid attention to my commands, your peace would have been like a river, your righteousness like the waves of the sea." How this verse touches my heart! I wasted so many years of my life. Only now can I truly live; it is never too late!

Jesus loves us more than we can possibly imagine. . I hope my story can help someone else. He is waiting to bring peace and righteousness to all in the bondage of sin, no matter your struggle. Give Him your "all in all," and just see what happens. I can promise it will be wonderful.

◆ Eric Barger's Testimony
Drugs, New Age, and now a Christian

I was the only child of two other "only" children. Due to my mother's advanced rheumatoid arthritis, we lived with her parents. When my dad and mom split up, my grandparents accepted the responsibility of raising me. I was raised going to church. Though I would have claimed to be a Christian, I had never trusted Jesus as the Lord and Savior of my life.

Early in my life, it became evident that I had musical talent. By age ten, I had begged my grandmother for a guitar and began taking lessons. I first made money playing music when a local disc jockey hired my band to play at an area teen dance. That was in early 1963 and I was only eleven years old. By the fall of 1964, our band was busy just about every weekend playing dances and parties. Getting up to go to church on Sunday morning quickly became a thing of the past. By the time I turned sixteen, I was playing in the largest party bar at Ohio University six nights a week. I had thrown off the upbringing that Grandma and Grandpa had tried to give me, exchanging it for sexual experiences, drugs and the rock n' roll lifestyle. The idea of going to our little church seemed a waste of time. Gran had tried to deal with me but I was out of control and not willing to listen.

At seventeen, with one girl pregnant and my 23 year-old girlfriend very upset, I split for the West Coast. By twenty-one, I was playing regularly in the Seattle area recording studios and bars. Life had become one big "high". Sex, drugs and rock n' roll were all I really cared about. Traveling with my band and spreading myself around to any willing groupies and taking mind expanding MDA, psychedelic mushrooms, and LSD became my daily staples. I was searching for reality in eastern mysticism - something now called "the New Age." I had a lingering affair with a bonafide practicing witch who dabbled in candle magic and astrology. I wanted to know why

I existed and where I was going, but my very existence was distorted and the forecast for my future was at best "cloudy with limited visibility."

With my search for reality at a dead end, I found myself burnt out, disillusioned and in a fog. I left the group and invested what I had into a recording studio. From that first small studio, I moved through several others and finally became the studio manager for what is now the largest state-of-the-art recording complex on the West Coast. I had found my niche.

It was at this point in my life that I met Melanie. At first, she was destined to be no more than another notch on my belt. But I really began to feel something different for her. After knowing her for only three weeks, I moved out of my girlfriend's house and did what I always said I'd never do - I got married!

Melanie and I had a lot in common. She had a library of reference books on witchcraft and the occult. We were both into partying, drugs, and rock n' roll. But the bliss didn't last. It wasn't long before Melanie found that I couldn't be satisfied with just her. But as far as I could understand what love was, I loved Melanie. What was I to do? We tried marriage counseling of the secular brand. After two visits, we both agreed that was a dead end. So on we went - drugging and drinking and partying and bickering.

One day during a heated argument, Melanie threw a two-inch thick phone directory of yellow pages at me. I had made a smart comment about getting our lives straightened out through a marriage counselor. Shaking off being nailed in the back of the head with the yellow pages, I picked them up, shook them at her, and for reasons unknown to me, I said, "But it's gotta be a Christian marriage counselor." She screamed, "You figure it out; you *@&$%!!" and slammed the bedroom door.

The next morning I opened those same yellow pages to "religious counselors," closed my eyes and jabbed my finger at the page. The number I hit was that of a real live, Bible-believing, Christian minister who counseled people from the office of his real estate firm.

During that first conversation with the counselor, he asked if we were "Christians". I said, "Oh sure." After three sessions with Ted, the counselor, I began making up any excuse possible to get out of going to see him. Melanie kept going and was genuinely seeking and receiving help.

I came home from the studio one evening in my usual state of being loaded on drugs to find a Bible sitting on the coffee table. Melanie began to read the Bible and supernaturally God slowly drew her to faith in Jesus. She stopped being my drug partner. She was different. But my life was still on a downward spiral. At one session, the counselor asked if either of us wanted to "receive Jesus as savior," Melanie said yes.

I'd had it. I promptly left her for several days, but as time passed, I missed her and our girls. So back I came to find that her witchcraft books were gone. Over the span of just a few days, she had become like the Apostle Paul's sister! But when she realized that preaching at me was not going to facilitate any change, she started loving me unconditionally, which was nearly unbearable.

Weeks passed, then months. We were still together, in theory, but it was anything but happy or peaceful. One Friday night she discovered my car close to a girlfriend's house. Though she didn't catch me there, I knew I'd been caught by the note she left on my windshield. Melanie spent the day praying and crying to God for direction. She and our counselor had prayed on the phone at 1 am "God ... whatever it takes ... GET ERIC!"

Sunday was a cold, rainy Seattle day. Melanie went to the bookstore to find something that would give her peace. Melanie says that I came home in a drunken state. She has had to help me accurately reconstruct this story. She says that I came through our front door screaming obscenities at her and began blaming her for all our problems. At some point I simply sat down on the floor and passed out. Two hours later I came to. I climbed up onto the couch where she had been sitting quietly praying for me. I was trying to find the words to inform her that I was finally going to divorce her when I picked up the book that was lying there between us. In my nervousness, I flipped open to page 60. There on the left side of the page, underlined with my wife's pen were three words: "GOD HATES DIVORCE!"

I finally reached out to God. I fell on the floor and burst into tears. I genuinely pleaded with God (and my wife) to forgive me. I was forgiven right there of every evil thing I had ever done. How am I sure? It is because the Bible promises that "whosoever calls on the name of the Lord SHALL BE SAVED" (Romans 10:13). I had searched enough for "inner enlightenment" to know that the answer to life didn't lie inside of me. For the first time, I had an inexpressible feeling of wholeness and value. I was clean. I was saved!

Our lives were radically changed! God called us into the ministry - to travel and warn people about the messages being sent through the lyrics and lifestyles of the Entertainment and Music worlds. We now teach how the New Age Movement offers "self enlightenment," but is only repackaged occultism in a humanist guise, and we train people how to effectively wage Spiritual Warfare. We've truly come "From Rock To THE Rock!"

I really wish my story were much different. More than once I have wrapped my arms around my now-grown daughters and asked their forgiveness for the things I did during their formative years, most of all for just neglecting to be a good, loving dad.

My mother passed away in 1989. I had been a Christian for over eight years. God gave me the precious opportunity to lead my mother to the Cross of Christ just nine months before she succumbed to cancer.

I also had many opportunities to talk with my beloved grandmother before her passing at 103 years in 2001. Through our many talks and tears, I was able to discern with all certainty that my grandmother did know Jesus personally. I will be forever grateful that time and again I was able to say "thanks" to her for being there for me.

http://www.ericbarger.com:80/rock.html
http://ericbarger.blogspot.com/

◆ Josh McDowell's Testimony
I was a skeptic but I knew what I wanted

Where I was brought up, many people had "religion." So I took off on religion. I was involved in it morning, afternoon, and night. However, I must have gone to the wrong church, because I actually felt worse.

Next I thought, "Well, maybe education is the answer." So I enrolled in the university. I was probably the most unpopular student with the professors in the first university I went to in Michigan. I wanted answers. My economics theory professor could tell me how to **make** a better living, but he couldn't tell me how to **live better**. It didn't take me long to realize that a lot of faculty members and students, too, had more problems, less meaning to life, and more frustration than I did.

Then I thought, "Maybe prestige is the answer." Find a "calling" and give your life to it. So I ran for various student body offices and got elected. It was neat... knowing everyone on campus, making decisions, spending other people's money to do what I wanted. I enjoyed it. But every Monday morning I woke up the same individual, usually with a headache because of the night before, with the same attitude, "Well, here we go again for another five days." Monday through Friday I sort of endured. So called 'happiness' revolved around finding 'fun' things to do three nights a week: Friday, Saturday, and Sunday. Then I'd start the whole cycle again.

Eventually I became frustrated. I doubt if too many students in the universities of our planet have been more sincere in trying to find meaning, truth, power and purpose in life than I was – yet I hadn't found it.

What's With These People?

About that time, around the campus I noticed a small group of people – eight students and two faculty. There was something different about their lives. They seemed to have direction. They appeared to know where they were going, and that was very unusual.

Further, they seemed to have a type of love that was manifested in the way they treated people. I had observed that most people *talked* a lot about love, but these people *demonstrated* something special in their relationships with others. They had something I didn't have, so, intrigued, I made friends with them.

After a couple of weeks, we were sitting around a table in the student union. I recall that six of the students were there and both of the faculty and one of their wives. The conversation started to get to God.

Let's face it: if you're an insecure student, professor, business-person, or an insecure anything, and the conversation gets to God, you have to put on a big front. You know what I've found to be true? The bigger the mouth, the greater the vacuum. The bigger the front an individual puts on, the greater the emptiness inside. Well, I was putting on that kind of front.

Their talk irritated me. I wanted what they had, but I didn't want them to know it. I leaned back on my chair and tried to act non-chalant. I looked over at one young woman and said, "Why are you so different from the other students on campus?" She said two words I never thought I'd hear in the university as part of the "solution." She said, "Jesus Christ."

"Oh, come on," I fired back at her. "Don't give me that garbage about religion." She must have had a lot of courage and convictions. "Look," she said, "I didn't tell you *religion*; I told you Jesus Christ." Well, I apologized to her because I'd been very rude... "Please forgive my attitude, but to tell you the truth, I'm sick and tired of that kind of thing. I just don't want anything to do with it."

Then you know what happened? These students and faculty challenged me to examine *intellectually* who Jesus Christ was. At first I thought it was a joke. How ridiculous. It was my opinion that most Christians had two brains. I thought one was lost and the other was out looking for it!

But these people kept challenging me over and over and over again, until finally I accepted their challenge.

The Search Continues

I spent a lot of time and money to completely discredit Christianity, but it backfired. I concluded that Christ had to be who He claimed to be. "You came to that conclusion intellectually?" you say.

That's right. Let me show you how. I concluded that if I could show that either one of two basic areas was not historically trustworthy or true, I had won my case against Christianity.

1. What about the Bible?

The first area: to demonstrate that the New Testament was not historically reliable. It was written years after Christ had died, I thought, and all those myths and legends had crept in, along with errors and discrepancies. That's all I had to do, but, as I said, it backfired.

When I speak in a literature or a history class now, I state that there is more evidence for the historical reliability of the New Testament than for any 10 pieces of classical literature *put together*. For example, when you study history, you need to develop a historiography, a proper approach to evaluating historical documents. There are three basics tests – the *bibliographic* test, the *internal evidence* test, and the *external evidence* test.

Let me just touch on the bibliographic test, which asks questions about manuscripts. A manuscript is a handwritten copy rather than a printed one. One question this test asks is how many manuscripts you have. The more manuscripts you have, the easier it is to reconstruct the original (referred to as the *autograph*) and check for errors or discrepancies.

Let me tell you what I found in relation to the New Testament. When I wrote the book *Evidence That Demands a Verdict* in 1974, I was able to document 14,000 manuscripts of just the New Testament (that's not counting the Old Testament). In the revised edition, I have been able to document 24,633 manuscripts of just the New Testament. By comparison, the Number Two book in manuscript authority in all history is the *Iliad* by Homer, which has 643 manuscripts.

2. ...and the Resurrection?

I felt the second area would be even simpler to discount. Everything that Jesus Christ taught, lived, and died for was based on His resurrection. All I had to do was prove that it never took place. However, that, too, backfired on me. What I discovered, in fact, led to my writing *The Resurrection Factor* because of the evidence.

Have you heard of Dr. Simon Greenleaf, who held the Royal Professorship of Law at Harvard? He was a world-renowned skeptic, often mocking the Christians in his classes. One day they challenged him to take the three volumes he had written on the laws of legal evidence and apply them to the resurrection. After much persuasion he did that. In the process he became a Christian and went on to write a book about his search. Greenleaf concluded that the resurrection of Jesus Christ is one of the best-established events in history according to the laws of legal evidence. Later he placed his personal faith in Jesus, the Messiah his Old Testament had promised would come.

The Problem of Will

So I had a problem. I found out that becoming a Christian (or I prefer the term a *believer*, or *follower of Christ*) was rather ego shattering.

My intellect was convinced, but a struggle began in my life. Jesus Christ directly challenged me to trust Him as Savior, as the One who died on the cross for my sins. "To all who received Him, to those who believed in His name, He gave the right to become children of God" (John 1:12). But I didn't want a "party pooper" invading my life. I couldn't think of a faster way to ruin a good time, destroy intellectual pursuits or impede scholarly acceptability with my peers.

My mind told me that Christianity was true; but my will said, "Don't admit it."

It came to the point where I'd go to bed at ten at night, but I couldn't fall asleep until four in the morning. I knew I had to get Jesus off my mind or go out of my mind!

New Life Begins

On December 19, 1959, at 8:30 p.m., during my second year at the university, I became a Christian.

That night I prayed. I prayed four things in order to establish a relationship with God – a personal relationship with His Son, the personal, resurrected, living Christ. Over a period of time, that relationship has turned my life around!

First, I prayed, "Lord Jesus, thank You for dying on the cross for me." Second, I said, "I confess those things in my life that aren't pleasing to You and ask You to forgive me and cleanse me." The Bible says, "Though your sins are like scarlet, they shall be as white as snow" (Isaiah 1:18). Third, I said, "Right now, in the best way I know how, I open the door of my heart and life and trust You as my Savior and Lord. Take control of my life. Change me from the inside out. Make me the type of person You created me to be."

The last thing I prayed was "Thank You for coming into my life by faith." It was a faith produced by the Holy Spirit, based on God's Word and supported by evidence and the facts of history.

I'm sure you've heard religious people talk about their "bolt of lightning." Well, after I prayed **nothing** happened emotionally or experientially. In fact, after I made that decision, I felt sick to my stomach.

"Oh no, McDowell, what'd you get sucked into now?" I wondered. I really felt I'd gone off the deep end – and some of my friends agreed.

Changes

But I can tell you one thing: In six months to a year and a half, I found I hadn't gone off the deep end. My life was changed.

A few years ago I was in a debate with the head of the history department at a mid-western university, and I said, "My life has been changed." He interrupted me rather sarcastically. "Mc-Dowell, are you trying to tell us that God really changed your life in the 20 century? What areas?"

After 45 minutes of my describing changes, he said, "Okay, that's enough."

Mental Peace. I told him about my restlessness. I was a person who always had to be occupied. I had to be over at my girlfriend's place or somewhere in a rap session. My mind was a whirlwind of conflicts. I'd sit down and try to study or think, and I couldn't.

But a few months after I made that decision to trust Christ, a kind of mental peace began to develop. Don't misunderstand, I'm not talking about the absence of conflict. What I found in this relationship with Jesus wasn't so much the absence of conflict as it was the ability to cope with it. I experience in a very real way Christ's promise when He said, "Peace I leave with you; My peace I give to you. I do not give to you as the world gives" (John 14:27).

Control of Temper. Another area that changed was my bad temper. I used to "blow my stack" if somebody just looked at me cross-eyed. I still have the scars from almost killing a man my first year at the university. My temper was such an integral part of me that I didn't consciously seek to change it.

One day after my decision to put my faith in Christ, I arrived at a crisis, only to find that my temper was gone! And only once in the many years since 1959 have I lost it.

A Man I Hated

There's another area that I'm not proud of. Hatred. It wasn't something outwardly manifested, but a kind of inner grinding. The one person I hated more than anyone else in the world was my father. I despised him. To me he was the town alcoholic.

If friends were coming over, I would take my father, tie him up in the barn, and park the family car up around the silo. To avoid embarrassment, we would tell our friend he had to go somewhere. I don't think any person could hate someone more than I hated my father.

Hatred Becomes Love

Maybe five months after I made that decision for Christ, love for my father – a love from God through Jesus Christ – inundated my life. It turned my hatred upside down. It enabled me to look my father squarely in the eyes and say, "Dad, I love you." After some of the things I'd done, that really shook him up.

When I transferred to a private university, I was in a serious car accident. With my neck in traction, I was taken home. I'll never forget my father coming into my room and asking, "Son, how can you love a father like me? I said, "Dad, six months ago I despised you." Then I shared with him my conclusions about Jesus Christ.

"Dad, I let Jesus come into my life. I can't explain it completely, but as a result of this relationship, I've found the capacity to love and accept not only you, but other people – just the way they are."

Forty-five minutes later one of the greatest thrills of my life occurred. Somebody in my own family, someone who knew me so well I couldn't pull the wool over his eyes, my own father, said to me, "Son, if God can do in my life what I've seen Him do in yours, then I want to give Him the opportunity." Right there my father prayed with me and trusted Christ.

Usually changes take place over several days, weeks, months ...even years. The life of my father was changed right before my eyes. It was as though somebody reached in and turned on a light bulb. I've never seen such a rapid change before or since. My father touched alcohol only once after that. He got it as far as his lips and that was it. He didn't need it anymore.

It Works

I've come to one conclusion. A relationship with Jesus Christ changes lives. You can ignorantly laugh at Christianity; you can mock and ridicule it. But it works! If you trust Christ, watch your attitudes and actions – because Jesus Christ specializes in changing lives, forgiving sin, removing guilt, bringing peace and something better than happiness … a deep and lasting joy.

It's Personal

I've shared how I personally responded to the claims of Christ. You, too, need to ask the local question: "What difference does all this evidence make to me? What difference does it make whether or not I believe Christ died on the cross for my sins and rose again?"

The answer is stated best by something Jesus said to a doubter named Thomas. He told him, "I am the way and truth and the life. No one comes to the Father, except through Me" (John 14:6).

You can trust God right now by faith through prayer. Prayer is talking with God. God knows your heart and is not as much concerned with your words as He is with the attitude of your heart. If you have never trusted Christ, you can do that right now.

The prayer I prayed was this: "Lord Jesus, I need You. Thank You for dying on the cross for all my sins. I open the door of my life and trust You as my Savior. Thank You for forgiving my sins and giving me eternal life. I choose to follow You now. Make me the kind of person You want me to be. Thank you for loving me. Thank You that I can trust You."

www.josh.org

◆ Pete Arunpullop's Testimony
Christ Transformed my Buddhist Heritage

My story may not be as interesting or extreme as the others'. But it sure has changed the way I look at everything in life. Without lovely people around me who have given me spiritual support, I would not have come to know Jesus. Therefore, I would like to start off by thanking special ones who have come into my life and led me to the light.

It all started four years ago when I came over from Thailand, the country which still has a low growth rate of Christianity. At that point in time, I thought that Christianity is all about big belly Santa Clause. As time had gone by, I had a better understanding of what life is all about and why love is the answer to every conflict existing in the world.

Raised as a Buddhist, I was told that life after death will be determined by the way I live my life. Unlike Buddhism, Christianity introduces me to loving God who has my whole life planned out. Believing in him, I am certain that my life after death will be peaceful and pleasant. Being in heaven with the loving Father and people I love so much, I can never wish for more.

As I examined Christianity, I compared it with Buddhism:

- Buddha taught that desire is the source of all suffering. Therefore, he contended, in order to eliminate suffering we must eliminate desire. Such a goal is obviously difficult to attain, since it requires *desiring* to eliminate *desire*. Jesus said, "Blessed are those who hunger and thirst for righteousness, for they will be filled" (Matthew 5:6). According to Jesus, then, the issue is having *right* desire, not eliminating desire altogether.
- One of the fundamental tenets that set Christianity apart from Buddhism is that God is *personal*. Buddhists believe that ultimate reality is an impersonal Void or Emptiness (*sunyata*). What are the implications or benefits of God's

being personal? He is able to love us. He can also hear and answer our prayers. And He can empathize with our suffering (Exodus 3:7; Hebrews 4:15). A Void would not be able to do such things.

- *Mahayana* Buddhism believes there are *many bodhisatt-vas*. Christianity believes there has been only *one incarnation* of the Son of God.

About two years ago, I decided to get baptized because I had quite a lot of things in my life that I knew I couldn't solve on my own and I needed something bigger than me to take over. So I asked for spiritual help from God and his son, Jesus. Then, three words I am told to keep in mind at all times are trust, faith, and love.

Even today, I am still amazed at how things played out so smoothly. It seems like God had planned every single detail which led me to know him better. Ever since my first day in The U.S. till today, I can see and feel God's work shaping me and guiding me. He is always there for me. All I have to do is open my heart and welcome him in.

(Pete is a student at the University of Kentucky)

◆ Dan Rosensohn's Testimony
I am a Messianic Jew

"Hear, O Israel: The LORD our God, the LORD is one. Love the LORD your God with all your heart and with all your soul and with all your strength." Deut. 6:4-5 (NIV)

I recall hearing the Rabbi say theses scriptures from the Bema (podium) growing up. I felt like we were given our instructions, but I also remember how much I loved God. You feel very lucky when you are called to do something that you already love to do, but it does make you more deliberate then before.

"Impress them on your children. Talk about them when you sit at home and when you walk along the road, when you lie down and when you get up. Tie them as symbols on your hands and bind them on your foreheads. Write them on the doorframes of your houses and on your gates." Deut. 6:7-9 (NIV)

You see my first memories of life go back to when I was three, but the first memories of Temple and God were at the age of seven. These scriptures were impressed upon me as a child. No, we did not wear the phylacteries in my home or Temple, but the concept of seeking God first was taught. By introducing children to God at an early age it lays a foundation they can build on. We have enough evidence today to see a world when we do not introduce children to a knowledge and relationship with God.

The Rabbi spoke about a Savior, a Prince of Peace. At that very young age I remember saying the Savior will fix all that is wrong. The world looked good from the outside, but there was still so much sadness and despair.

In my case I did not follow God as I should have through the tough adolescent and early adult years. But I believe that commitment I made to God as a boy protected me, as if he was preserving me for another reason, one that I was not aware of.

There was another influence in my life as well, my father, he was a Professor and constantly challenged my ways of thinking.

He introduced me or challenged me to find Truth in life. I mean he wanted me to understand that there was an essence to life that most people know nothing about; you had to seek this "real meaning" in order to find it.

When my life began to unravel, although I knew of God as a small boy I did not continue to grow in God as I grew in the world. I was sincere in seeking the truth yet I was sincerely wrong in what I found. I will never forget my first encounter with Christ. I would feel overwhelmed and have a hard time coping with everyday life, a form of worrying and depression.

What is the first thing you should do when you find yourself in a situation like that? Pray. Well I would pray to God and it would sometimes take months for the littlest prayer to be answered. I shared this burden with someone and I asked, "What do you do when you feel that way"? They told me that they pray and asked Jesus to lift their burden. I was not afraid; after all, I was seeking for the Truth. I said that simple prayer, "Jesus lift these burdens off of me." No sooner did the prayers leave my lips, I felt the genuine lifting of my burdens.

"Come to me, all you who are weary and burdened, and I will give you rest. Take my yoke upon you and learn from me, for I am gentle and humble in heart, and you will find rest for your souls. For my yoke is easy and my burden is light." Matthew 11:28-30 (NIV)

I saw the power in the name of Jesus, I prayed to the Father through the Son, I acknowledged God's Son, and he answered my prayer.

"I have declared to both Jews and Greeks that they must turn to God in repentance and have faith in our Lord Jesus." (Acts 20:21 (NIV)

While in the world I sought after the good things that this world had to offer, the good things in this world will not bring you peace and eternal life. You must acknowledge to God that you were wrong in your thinking and seek him and ask him into your heart.

"But your iniquities have separated you from your God; your sins have hidden his face from you, so that he will not hear." (Isaiah 59:2 (NIV

"You will seek me and find me when you seek me with all your heart." (Jeremiah 29:13 (NIV)

"For there is no difference between Jew and Gentile--the same Lord is Lord of all and richly blesses all who call on him." Peace be with you! (Romans 10:12 (NIV)

Dan is an elder at Hill-n-Dale Christian Church

◆ James K. Walker's Testimony
I was a 4th generation Mormon

I was born and raised a Mormon – fourth-generation on my father's side. I was told that my ancestors were among the first converts to the Church of Jesus Christ of Latter-day Saints in north Florida. I was baptized at the age of eight and received the "laying on of hands" for the gift of the Holy Ghost. As a young man I received the Aaronic Priesthood serving in the offices of deacon, teacher, and priest. I later received a "temple recommend" and performed "Baptism for the Dead" in the Mormon Temple in Salt Lake City.

I believed with all of my heart that that Joseph Smith, Jr., was a prophet of God, that the Book of Mormon was the Word of God, and that the Church of Jesus Christ of Latter-day Saints was the only true church on the face of the earth.

I was fascinated by the story of the Prophet Joseph Smith. I tried to imagine what it was like for Joseph as a fourteen-year-old young man to have been visited by Heavenly Father and Jesus in the year 1820. The Savior told Joseph not to join any of the churches because they were all wrong and their beliefs were an abomination to Him. Joseph learned that there had been a "total apostasy" shortly after the death of the twelve apostles in the First Century. Thus, there was no true religion or gospel on the whole earth for almost seventeen hundred years until Joseph Smith was able to "restore" the true Gospel. I was taught that happened just ten years later in 1830 when Joseph reestablished the one True Church with six charter members.

I remember my father giving me my first copy of the Book of Mormon. He told me the story of the Angel Moroni who appeared in Joseph Smith's bedroom in 1823. Before restoring the Gospel, Joseph Smith was told about an ancient record of Jewish people who once lived in America. They had migrated from Jerusalem in a boat and sailed all the way to the Americas. Once here they multiplied and became two great nations – the

Nephites and the Lamanites. God sent them prophets, I was told, to call them to repentance and obedience. These Jewish people eventually became the principle ancestors of the Native American Indians.

One of the Nephite Prophets, Moroni, returned from the dead to tell Joseph Smith about the sacred Golden Plates that contained the scriptures of his people engraved in Reformed Egyptian Hieroglyphics. Joseph was eventually able to re-cover these gold plates from the Hill Cumorah near his home in Palmyra, New York and translate them into English by the "gift and power of God" before publishing the scripture as the Book of Mormon. I felt blessed to think how the words of the Prophets were preserved through the centuries and passed down through my father and now to me. I was also told of the other Scriptures in addition to the Bible and Book of Mormon that Joseph Smith received from God – the Doctrine & Covenants and the Pearl of Great Price.

I wanted to learn the Scriptures and be pleasing to God. More than anything else, I wanted to be like my Father in Heaven. I was taught that before He received "Celestial Exaltation," God, our Heavenly Father, was once a man who lived on some other "Earth." He was a worthy man, obedient to *His* Father in Heaven keeping the eternal principles and laws. Thus after He died, He and His wife, our Mother in Heaven, progressed to Godhood and became our Heavenly Parents. My priesthood leaders taught me that like earthly parents, Heavenly Father and Heavenly Mother, are blessed to give birth to children in heaven whom they love very much. I was taught that before coming to earth, each of us – the whole population of the earth – were born to our Heavenly Parents and lived with them before being born to our other parents here on earth. It was our spiritual responsi-bility, I believed, to return to them.

My goal was to be obedient to the principles of the Restored Gospel. I hoped to be able to find a wife who was a worthy member of the Church so that we could qualify to be married in the temple. A "Temple Marriage" I was promised, was not "until death till you part" but for "time and all eternity." By being a "Temple Mormon" and keeping the "laws and ordinances," I hoped that I would be worthy to attain the highest heaven – the Celestial Kingdom. I knew that although they were glorious, the lower heavens (the Terrestrial and Telestial Kingdoms) were destinations reserved for my brothers and sisters who did not achieve their potential.

My Priesthood leaders explained to me that because of Christ's atonement, those of us who were obedient and worthy could be like God. If we reached our spiritual potential, my wife and I would then become a God and Goddess and be as heavenly parents procreating our own spirit children to populate our own planet. Before he was God, our Heavenly Father was a man. He achieved Celestial Exaltation and has given us the same potential. As the Mormon Prophet Lorenzo Snow taught, "As man is, God once was; As God is, man may become."

I had the first clue that something might be wrong when I was in seventh grade. I had a Christian friend, Tommy, who looked up "Mormonism" in the encyclopedia. Tommy told me that we Latter-day Saints believed in a different God than Christians do. I bristled at that idea. I explained that we Mormons believe in the same God he did – we only had more information about Him from the Book of Mormon. Tommy then told me that he had looked it up in the encyclopedia which reported the Mormon teaching that God was once a man and the men could become Gods.

I told Tommy that we believe that – just like all the churches do. (I thought everyone believed that God was once a man). Tommy said that was one huge difference. He said that the Bible taught that there was only one true God and that every other god was a false god. I still remember him showing me in the Bible where God said, "… before me there was no God formed, neither will there be after me" (Isaiah 43:10). While I didn't fully understand the implications of that passage, the Lord used that verse and Tommy's testimony to plant a seed in my heart.

Years later I had some other Christian friends who shared their faith in a careful and kind way – asking me questions about my faith that really made me think. I also had some bad experiences with some Christians who were less than kind but, fortunately, such "bashing" was rare in my experience. I was eventually exposed to some of Joseph Smith's prophecies in the Doctrine & Covenants that failed (Deut 18:20-22). I remember my dismay to discover that the Book of Mormon, which I had been told had never been altered, had actually been changed in over 4,000 places since it was first published in 1830.

My questions about my church and my faith deepened into doubts. I began to wonder if Joseph Smith had really been visited by Heavenly Father and Jesus. I also began to feel insecure about my own salvation. I remember thinking, "How do I know if my sins are forgiven?" and "How do I know if I will return to Heavenly Father when I die?"

When I was 21, these spiritual questions festered into a real crisis as God began to confront me with my sin and lack of belief. My whole life I believed that Jesus Christ was the Savior of the world but it was like God was showing me that I was never truly trusting Christ as my Savior and Lord. I had been taught that Christ's atonement made my salvation and exaltation possible but it was my obedience that determined if I would be fully saved and in the presence of God in eternity. Even back in third grade, I had memorized Joseph Smith's *Articles of Faith*, one of which says, "We believe that through the atonement of Christ, all mankind may be saved by obedience to the laws and ordinances of the gospel." In my heart I knew I was not fully obeying all of God's laws even on my best day. The Book of Mormon teaches, "For we know it is by grace we are saved, after all we can do" (Nephi 25:23). But was I really doing all I could do?

The Lord touched my heart and for the first time I understood that God's grace meant that salvation was a free gift based on Christ's goodness and not my own – Christ's death burial and resurrection and not my good deeds or obedience. It was while I was still a sinner that Christ died on the cross to fully pay the penalty for my sins (Romans 5:8). If I was trusting my own obedience then I was not truly trusting the Lord Jesus Christ as my savior.

That November night God touched my heart and I repented of my sins and received eternal life as God's free gift. I now know that my sins have been forgiven and that I have already received eternal life (1 John 5:13). God radically changed my life through Christ my Lord. The life I live now I live for Christ who loved me and gave His life for me (Galatians 2:20).

James K. Walker currently serves as President of Watchman Fellowship, Inc., an evangelical Christian discernment ministry providing research, apologetics, and evangelism in the field of new religions movements, cults, the occult and counterfeit Christianity. He has a BA in Biblical Studies and an MA in Theology from Criswell College in Dallas. He speaks at churches, seminaries and universities throughout the US and internationally and is the author of the book The Concise Guide to Today's Religions and Spirituality. Contact James Walker at JWalker@watchman.org.

◆ Paul Blizard's Testimony
The Inside Story of a Former 3rd Generation Jehovah's Witness

To the average person, the name "Jehovah's Witnesses" brings to mind a group of neatly dressed people going from door to door in the neighborhood, leaving the Watchtower magazine, or perhaps a book. However, when I think of Jehovah's Witnesses, I recall a lifetime of bondage to a cult which I served for the first 28 years of my life. My grandfather, son of a Baptist minister, became a part of the Watchtower Society in the early 1900s.

I was taught that Jehovah's Witnesses were the only true religion. It is a religion governed from Watchtower headquarters in Brooklyn, New York. The controlling council or "Governing body" is comprised of a handful of elderly men who control the lives of over eight million people. Jehovah's Witnesses are taught that everything written by Watchtower leaders is from God Himself and is never to be questioned. They believe that the Governing body receives what they call, "new light" from angelic beings which explain their unique Bible teachings. This angelic information is passed on to the rank and file in printed form through Watchtower printed materials. They believe the Watchtower organization is the sole agency on the earth God is using. So, according to them, apart from the Watchtower organization, people have no hope. Jehovah's Witnesses believe they alone have what they call "the truth." They also believe they alone are the only true Christians, which means, they alone will be saved. All others are considered part of "Babylon the Great-the world empire of false religion." All church members and others will be slaughtered by Jehovah God at the battle of Armageddon.

I began full-time Watchtower service in 1971 after dropping out of High School with the encouragement of Watchtower leaders. They had predicted the end of the world to occur in 1975. During this era, thousands of Jehovah's Witnesses cashed in insurance policies, abandoned careers, and sold their possessions to spend the "short time remaining" in the ministry work before the end of the world. As a missionary worker or "Pioneer," I went from door to door trying to convince people that they must become Jehovah's Witnesses to please God and perhaps receive salvation.

I use the word "perhaps" because all Jehovah's Witnesses are not sure of their salvation. The Watchtower's way of salvation is based upon works, rather than the saving grace of Jesus Christ, which through faith we freely receive.

Each Jehovah's Witness must fill out monthly reports recording time spent in their proselytizing work to the elders. Elders put the information into a personal file. There are files kept on each member of the congregation. Secret files are also kept which also contain sensitive information regarding any major sins or infractions of rules and personal habits of individuals. These secret files related to a Witness' private life are transferred to master files at the New York City headquarters. These files are never destroyed.

Since I had been living in this system all my life, I knew what was expected of me. I had to follow the rules and laws to gain salvation. I had been going from door to door since I was a small child, so I adapted to full-time service easily.

I continued such service for a number of years, but with little satisfaction. The burden of keeping up with the monthly quotas of 100 hours of time, as well as sales of a minimum of 100 magazines and 40 books, started to discourage me. All of this work is voluntary and there are no salaries paid. Witnesses must find employment that will support this work. (Quotas vary from year to year).

In 1973, I was invited to go to the World Headquarters in Brooklyn to be part of the vast staff of workers who produce the literature. In a personal letter from the president of The Watchtower Society, Nathan H. Knorr, he stated: "Additionally, you are going to get a wonderful four-year advanced theocratic training which is far better than any secular education you can get."

With much anticipation I boarded a plane for New York City. While on the plane I recalled all my friends' envy, in that I was going to be living with the Governing body members, and how grand it would be to be at the hub of all the activity of the work around the world. My friends gave me going-away parties and gifts, commending my proud parents on raising me in the organization so well that they could see their son go to such a place.

Soon after arriving in New York, the illusion wore off as I was assigned to work in the factory. Hard labor and learning the ways of the organization from the inside out was the "education" I obtained at Watchtower headquarters. Space does not permit details of what I experienced while spending long hours working in the book bindery. There I operated equipment for "God's organization." I recall the mental stress of a profusion of rules and regulations. The master plan of the Watchtower leaders controlled where we went, what we did, and how we did it.

After spending three years at headquarters, with no money to start out in the world (our pay was $14.00 (U.S.) per month), I learned the harsh reality of trying to make a living with no training or skills. Jehovah's Witnesses are strongly discouraged from attending college. I married a good Jehovah's Witness girl, and we set out together trying to please God the best way we knew how. That is, we were good Jehovah's Witnesses and followed all the rules and laws. My wife had been a missionary for eight years. Pat had been sent to different parts of the United States in her work, under the direction of the Watchtower Society.

After I returned home with a fairly "clean file" from the New York office, the local elders were using me quite extensively in teaching from the platform. Most Jehovah's Witnesses agree that anyone who has spent any time at headquarters is special and worthy of greater responsibilities in the local congregation.

As I gained status in the congregation, I was being exposed to and trained in some of the undercover work of the local elders. It was exciting slinking around in the darkness, spying on members of the congregation who were suspected of wrongdoing. I also was given access to the congregation files, which revealed the inside information of all in the congregation. I was being used in the same kind of covert operations I had seen control the workers at headquarters.

Through all this I could not receive any satisfaction and peace. The pressure of trying to serve a God who is vengeful and full of wrath is more than I can describe. The organization always painted a picture of Jehovah as a God ready to "pour out vengeance." All I knew of God was what I read in the Watchtower. Yes, we did read the Bible, but were told that if we did so apart from the Watchtower books to interpret it, we were destined to fall into apostasy and ultimately be destroyed by God.

A friend introduced me to a book that was written by a former Jehovah's Witness called "Thirty Years a Watchtower Slave." I knew that my duty as a good Witness was to turn in my friend to the elders, for we were forbidden to read any anti-Witness material.

But in defiance, I read the book. It disturbed me greatly, for the author was a former worker at headquarters, and I could relate to many of the things he was saying. Many things that I had tried to erase from my memory were surfacing again, and questions of the Watchtower's authority left me very unsettled. The author mentioned that he had found the truth by studying the Bible apart from Watchtower publications.

All this time I believe God was leading us to study His Word alone apart from books. Even though we had our own New World Translation of the Bible (translated by the Watchtower Society and refuted by Hebrew and Greek scholars as being a biased, twisted version of the Bible), we bought a New American Standard Bible.

My wife and I secretly studied our new Bible long hours into the night, discovering that many of the major doctrines that we had been willing to die for were false. I shared with my father some of the things I had discovered. Being an elder, my father saw that I was questioning some of their main teachings, and he reported my wife and me to the elders, to stand trial for apostasy.

After a lengthy, tearful hearing, we repented of doubting the Watchtower Society and were allowed to remain as Jehovah's Witnesses, but I was stripped of all my responsibilities in the congregation. I was to be watched for a period of time before serving in any capacity in the congregation again. All this information was noted on our files.

A job transfer to another town was a welcome relief. We looked forward to entering another congregation and getting a fresh start. But soon the disappointment came when we remembered that the details of our trial were in our files and would follow us wherever we went for the rest of our lives!

They warned us they would excommunicate us if we tried to share such ideas with anyone in the congregation. We vowed loyalty to the organization, and said we would not read or speak about anything that would be different from the Watchtower's position on Scripture.

Two years passed. Being under the elders' scrutiny left us very empty. Nothing, not even our children who had brought us so much joy, made our lives fulfilling. We had a need for something, but what it was we did not know. We would drink to excess often, searching for some kind of joy, but only emptiness resulted.

Having two boys, we longed for a girl to be born and hoped that having a little girl would complete the happiness missing from our family. On Aug. 10, 1980, Jenny Leigh Blizard was born. We were so excited but tragedy struck. At five weeks old, Jenny received a small cut on a finger which would not stop bleeding. Local doctors found that Jenny's blood simply would not clot.

They sent us to San Antonio, Texas, for treatment of Jenny's condition. She was admitted to Santa Rosa Medical Center's special care nursery, looking for the treatment that would make Jenny well. Doctors worked feverishly trying to reach a diagnosis.

Finally, a team of doctors informed us that Jenny needed an emergency blood transfusion to save her life. This was a difficult problem for us because Watchtower law does not permit any Jehovah's Witness to take blood in any form. Jehovah's Witnesses carry cards stating that under no circumstances will they take a transfusion, even if it means death.

We sent the doctors out of the room and told them that we would give them our answer soon. My wife and I prayed and cried out to God for answers. I remember thinking; "Oh Jehovah, how can you ask me to make such a decision - a yes or no whether Jenny lives or dies! What kind of God are you!" Finally my wife and I called the doctors back into the room, and we informed them that we had to obey God's law and we would have to let Jenny die.

The hospital officials contacted the Texas Child Welfare Dept. and a suit was filed against us for child abuse and neglect. A court order was issued to ensure that Jenny would receive the blood she needed to save her life. The Sheriff's Department of Bexar County issued us citations and warned the hospital staff not to allow us to remove Jenny from the hospital. They knew full well that Jehovah's Witnesses have a long history of sneaking patients out of hospitals to avoid blood transfusions at all costs.

My wife and I were secretly relieved that Jenny would get the care she needed to save her life. We felt we had done all we could in trying to stop them from giving her the blood. We never thought the courts would intervene.

In the meantime, friends contacted the local elders, who promptly came to visit us. They were relieved to find out that there was still time to plan a way to kidnap Jenny out of the hospital before blood could be administered.

I explained to them that the matter was out of my hands and that I was under court order not to remove Jenny. That did not matter to them. Their main concern was to get her out.

I knew that Jenny would shortly die if I removed her from the machines that were keeping her alive, and I would be charged with murder. I explained this to the elders. They replied, "That's the chance you have to take! You cannot allow them to give your child blood!"

Without further discussion, I asked them to leave, stating that we could not allow our child to die in this way. "If this is the God I serve, I am through with Him."

The elders left the hospital angry that we would not submit to their demands "I hope," one elder even said, "She gets hepatitis from that blood, just to prove that it's bad!"

When we finally returned home with Jenny, the Witnesses had received word that even though we had protested the transfusion, we "allowed" her to take it. This made us outcasts in their eyes. They did not excommunicate us because their law calling for expulsion would have applied only if we had freely given permission for the transfusion.

This is when we feel God stepped in. Local Christians came to our home and helped us out with food and helpful aid. The living testimony of these people affected my wife and me so much that we decided to start again studying the Bible.

Those months of intense secret study of the Bible led us to conclude we had lived a lie. We had been in bondage to a system of interpretation of scripture which squelched any free thinking. On the issues and doctrinal points that I had so much trouble, the Bible was clear. I read the Bible in context, without the aid of books or magazines to instruct us.

The result of this study was that we found all we needed for Salvation was faith in the Lord Jesus Christ. We also found that He is a God of love.

One night, my wife and I held hands and gave our lives to the Lord Jesus Christ. Suddenly, we felt a release in our spirit, a release that brought freedom, liberty, and salvation. We were, as Jesus said: "born again." I had never had a feeling like it in all the thousands of hours I had spent striving to please God as a good Jehovah's Witness. We knew that we were changed. We were a "new creation." As the Apostle John said: "These things have I written unto you that believe on the name of the Son of God; that ye may know that ye have eternal life, and that ye may believe on the name of the Son of God." (I John 5:13)

Of course, we were promptly disfellowshipped from the Jehovah's Witness religion. Under the rules of our excommunication, we cannot have contact with any of our family and life long friends in the organization. Our own parents and family members will not be allowed to go to our funerals. According to the Watchtower law, we are to be regarded as dead. Any Witnesses caught talking to us is subject to judicial action, including disfellowshipping.

In conclusion, I must say that we are not dead, but very much alive. Yes, we are dead to a former way of life, but alive in Jesus Christ, full of the Holy Spirit and power, saved by the blood of the Lamb!

Jenny's condition was more serious than what a transfusion could permanently correct. The transfusions given to her as an infant did prolong her life, but on March 3, 1987, our six- year-old Jenny went home to be with the Lord. On Jenny's memorial stone it is inscribed: "God's special messenger." We believe she truly was. Through her illness and brief life, we came to recognize the deception of the Watchtower Society, profess and receive Jesus Christ as Lord and Savior and share this redemptive knowledge with Jehovah's Witnesses around the world.

In addition, during the final 39 days of Jenny's life, in Dallas' Children's Medical Center, My wife and I spent much of our time praying and testifying for Christ with families of other serious and terminally ill children at the hospital.

Finally, some details of Jenny's funeral attest to the evil nature of the Watchtower Society and the control it holds over its members. At Jenny's funeral, the first four pews were reserved for family members. The remaining rows of pews were open to church family and local townspeople. The latter were packed. People from all over came to share in the grief of the loss of this small child. However, the pews set aside for Jenny's family were occupied by only four people -- Myself, my wife Pat, and Jenny's two brothers. No other family members attended the funeral. They were ordered not to by Watchtower leaders. The callousness shown by the Watchtower Society in forbidding relatives from attending the service is deplorable.

In 2007 my father passed away. Not one family member called to let me know of his death.

Our prayer is through our testimony those caught in religious bondage will wake up to the freedom found only in the person of Jesus Christ.

Let me encourage anybody who is thinking of the "losses" if they abandon the Watchtower to follow Jesus Christ. There is a price to pay, there is a cost. Yes, your Jehovah's Witness friends will not speak to you, perhaps even your own family will leave you as orphans. However, if you give your life to Jesus Christ, you will have a heavenly Father who will supply all your needs and then some! Psalm 27:10 says "For my father and my mother have forsaken me, but the LORD will take me up." Since we left the Watchtower, we have made hundreds of wonderful friends and have a church family who love us. You are in for blessings you cannot even imagine. One Bible text which has become special to us recently is, Job 42:10: "The LORD restored the fortunes of Job when he prayed for his friends, and the LORD increased all that Job had *twofold*." Yes the loss of a child is devastating; however we have received a twofold blessing. In December of 2002 we adopted twin orphan girls from Russia. Our new daughters are truly gifts from God. Trust in God, believe in Him, and let Him take care of the details! Watch for my new book coming out. It's all about five generations who were severely affected by the Watchtower teaching.

Paul Blizard
Pastor of Memorial Baptist Church
Beckley, West Virginia

◆ Orpah Hicks' Testimony (co-author of this book)
I was a cultural Christian until Jesus touched my life

I was born in rural Kentucky. My family defined being a Christian as a person believing in God, family, being patriotic, and being a community servant. My grandfather was elected to the office of County Judge and Sheriff. He served as Superintendent of our County's Schools and was a carpenter by trade. My father was an electrical engineer and many teachers were within the family.

My recall is going to church periodically while living at home and involvement in youth group while attending a mountain mission boarding school. I knew God was important and feared hell. I was baptized at age eleven but my life never changed. When occasionally thinking about right and wrong, I hoped to earn God's approval by doing more good than bad. I had no clue as to who Jesus is, what he has done for mankind or that I could have a relationship with him. In growing up in an Appalachian community I saw poverty, felt many kinds of pain, suffering and hurt; observed alcohol's destructiveness, lived through my parents divorce, witnessed the tragic death of my great grandmother, and was alone with my grandfather when he died of a heart attack. By the time I had married and given birth to my only child I became over whelmed with life. In spite of my best efforts, I felt that I was failing to be a good wife and mother.

Desperate for answers to questions I did not even know how to ask, I began going to church regularly and studying the Bible. The Scripture that first spoke to my scattered ness and confusion was Matthew 6:33... *"Seek first the kingdom of God and His righteousness and all these things shall be added to you."* This established a point of beginning and would set my priorities in proper order. As a result I learned that we all live in a fallen world and that all people are sinful including me. As taught in the Scriptures, I repented of my sin of *running my own life apart from God* and asked Jesus to be my Savior and

Lord. Sometime afterward, as I lay on my bed filled with anxiety, my eyes were opened to understand what Jesus had done on the cross was for me. He had paid my personal sin debt! I was filled with many emotions. One of which was the overwhelming feeling of gratitude and wonder as I began to absorb the significance of something I had never understood before in my life! During that time my life was changed having a new purpose and direction. I had a burning desire to understand God's Word. I could not be a mere pew sitter, and do nothing. I became very goal oriented. My number one goal in raising my daughter was that she too would come to have a relationship with God. Life became a challenge to live in relationship with God and it became an opportunity to serve others. Through my life's struggles, fears and burdens, God strengthened me and my life became rooted and stable – not trouble free. God placed a desire in my heart to do whatever I could to help other young women who were struggling and searching just like me. At this time of thanking God and having a compelling concern for others in my same situation I never dreamed what my life would look like today. I was not educated to be a teacher and knew absolutely nothing about the Bible. Yet, I have become a student of the Scriptures, written Bible lessons and taught Bible for about 35 years. God has opened many doors of opportunity to serve:

- as a leader in women's ministries in my church
- served as Greater Lexington Christian Women's Club Chairman and other CWC positions
- Stonecroft Ministries – CWC speaker
- Stonecroft Ministries - Central Ky Area Rep
- Stonecroft Ministries - Central Ky FBC Coordinator
- served in our city committee for the city's "Franklin Graham Festival"
- served in the city committee for the city's "Just Give Me Jesus Conference" with Ann Graham Lotz
- currently co-authoring this book

As I look back over my life, the only explanation I have for doing these things is by the enabling power of the Holy Spirit whom all believers receive, when they ask Jesus to be Lord of their life. What a privilege that God would use an ordinary Kentucky girl, raised in the Appalachian Mountains – doing such things for His kingdom. I have no idea how many bible classes that I have been privileged to guide or the number of times I have spoken for Christian Women's Club Meetings. While serving as Stonecroft's FBC Coordinator, we had around 75 active Bible studies in the central KY area.

Another highlight in my ministry was when I was given the opportunity to teach at the North American Christian Convention in Indianapolis, IN. I also participated in the counselor training program for the "Just Give Me Jesus Conference" when Ann Graham Lotz spoke in Lexington, KY.

My husband Sam and I have been married for 47 years. We are blessed to have a devoted Christian daughter and son-in-law, whom we love like a son. They have given us three grandchildren whom they are presently nurturing in the faith.

◆ Jean Eason's Testimony (co-author of this book)
Why I left Jehovah's Witnesses

I was a third generation Jehovah's Witness (JW) – (followers of the Watchtower Bible and Tract Society). We truly believed we could not earn eternal life unless we attended all meetings at the Kingdom Hall (KH), witnessed from house to house, make return visits and start a "Bible" study with them in their home (it was really a JW book study). Our goal was to convince the people we called on that we "JWs" had the "Truth" and they must also become a JW to have eternal life (we truly believed we were the only ones who had the Truth). We were to encourage them to attend all the meetings at the KH and as soon as they were ready, teach them how to go from house to house and leave the Watchtower (WT) literature (for a donation) and do the same thing.

We did not celebrate holidays and birthdays. Every word written by the WT was considered "truth" that must be followed to the letter, whether it's taking a blood transfusion, voting, participating in war, saying a pledge to the flag or attending a place of worship other than the KH. To do otherwise was sinning against Jehovah, resulting in the possibility of losing their hope of eternal life.

I was married and had three children before I began having serious doubts about the WT being God's *only* channel of communication. These doubts began to emerge as the WT printed "new light" (a change in their previous teaching) in their publications. I wondered, "Why did Jehovah change His mind?" I held this thought as a series of events began to take place.

Witnesses are instructed to inform their doctors about their abstaining from blood transfusions. We signed papers relieving the doctors and hospital of all responsibility should our babies die from needing blood. I had an Rh factor blood condition and in those days they transfused the baby at birth should a problem occur. Fortunately, I was spared - but I was ready and willing to let my children die! Why? Because I was convinced that the WT had the "Truth" and should I do differently, I would lose the hope of eternal life and so would my child.

One of the WT changes led us to believe that should we see JWs sinning and do not report them, you are guilty of that sin yourself. A sister in our congregation took blood when she hemorrhaged at childbirth. My options were to report her and if I didn't, the sin fell on me. Both options bothered me! You see, when you are uninformed of having a relationship with Christ, you follow people blindly, trusting them to be in God's will. Like a good JW, I reported her and she had to appear before a committee of elders. She was put on probation. I praise God she is out now and knows the Lord! This, along with other "new light" caused me to start thinking about "where and how" they get their new light!

I inherited a WT library from one of my relatives, and began reading the older publications. I learned they had changed their interpretation many times. I took note that the modern literature quoted often from the older publications. Now I was able to pick up the very book they quoted from - and guess what? They often misquoted - took out of context - and misapplied their own writings! After two years of research I realized I was following an organization led by man's interpretation of the Bible. I studied my way out!

I stopped attending meetings, and all JW activities, but entered a state of spiritual loneliness. Where could I go if all religions are false? Who has the "Truth?" After a great deal of reading books about the different denominations and how they were started, we began attending a Christian Church. We enjoyed being there to a degree but still not knowing for sure if it was of God or the devil. After all - all churches believe in the concept of the Trinity, hellfire, and a soul leaving the body at death. I didn't believe any of these doctrines! While I was trying desperately to sort out doctrines, the WT got "new light" saying if any JW attended church, they would be disfellowshiped. Not knowing whether we were following Satan or Jesus - we submitted to the elders, when called to a JW committee meeting. We stopped attending church - we were not ready to be disfellowshipped and be cut off from family and friends for something we were not yet sure of. Oh – how I yearned for *truth*! I continued to read and search.

Fifteen years later, my sister-in-law invited me to a special meeting to hear an out-of-town speaker. I had noticed a change in her life as she was talking about "knowing" Jesus. She was giving up bad habits such as smoking - she was aglow with something. I didn't know what (but of course it was the Holy Spirit!). The speaker shared the love of Jesus in a way that I'd never heard before. Oh, how I needed this message! When he finished, he asked that we stand, join hands, and sing the Lord's Prayer. Something much unexpected happened to me. Suddenly, I felt God's liquid love pour over me from the top of my head to the tip of my toes! Without knowing what had happened, I instantly realized I had been searching for "the truth" in all the wrong places. I had been searching for what was the truth instead of who was the Truth. Only the Holy Spirit can teach this way! Suddenly, I understood what the song meant, "He was there all the time"! John 14:6 says, "I am the way, the truth and the life, no man comes to the Father except by me." Yes, Jesus is the Truth and "He was there all the Time!" Also, I thought of another song, "He Touched Me." Oh how I wanted to rejoice but I restrained myself thinking people would notice a strange look on my face! I didn't know "Who" the Holy Spirit was, but I experienced Him!

When we left, my friend said, "How did you like it?" I just started laughing — I couldn't retain it in any longer! She said, "Something happened to you, didn't it?" I replied, "Yes I can't explain it — but I feel as though I've been cleansed inside and out!" I realize now that I was touched by the power of the Holy Spirit. God knew I could never find *the Truth* by searching through the definitions of words like "soul, hell, and Trinity." I had my Watchtower blinders on - I couldn't believe the simple gospel, I had to experience it!

I thought sure my new-found joy would be gone the next morning, but it wasn't! I woke up anxious to read the Bible and pray! As I read through the book of John, I wondered when the word "Jesus" was added to so many pages - seems like I had never seen that before! On my knees in the privacy of my living room, I asked Jesus to come into my life - I would do *anything* He asked of me. Well, don't pray this prayer if you're not willing - for I had no idea what He had in store!

My husband liked the change in me - then he was willing to visit prayer meetings, and finally, church. (Yes, we were reported by a JW when seen going into a church - we were visited by two JW elders telling us we were being disfellowshipped - yes - after being out for fifteen years)! Since then, this practice has stopped, but the end results are the same - they are still ostracized. My husband accepted Jesus as his Lord and Savior. The next year was spent in deprogramming ourselves - we had to learn *everything* over! Then the Lord put it on my heart to write a book of my testimony. I had no idea why I had kept all my research when reading the old WT literature, but now I had it for the book I was to write. It is now on line: www.tutorsforchrist.org. I was invited to appear on national TV along with three other former JWs. Soon, all of us began receiving a ton of mail! I had not expected to go into ministry any more than I expected to write a book — but here I was, living out my promise, "I'll do *anything*!" Before I knew it, I was sharing my research and my learned orthodox views with hundreds of JWs and Christians who needed to help loved ones in the JWs. I became a Christian discipler overnight! My JW discipline skills came in handy! I feel so very privileged to lead many JWs to Christ — it was such a joy to explain to them who the true person of Jesus Christ *really* is! (JWs believe Jesus is Michael the archangel — that he was Jehovah's first heavenly creation). The concept of the Trinity is very offensive to them. JWs make good witnesses for Jesus when they are converted to the *real Truth*!

As I have co-authored this book I'm amazed how God has worked in our lives. My husband, Bill and I have done things we never dreamed would be possible. Betty Stephens, Bill and I went to Ecuador and helped missionary Bill McDonald hold a seminar for the local pastors – while there, I shared my testimony in many churches that he had started. Bill McDonald was our first pastor in Lexington prior to going to Ecuador.

Through our ministry, Tutors for Christ, we conducted many conferences in and around Lexington helping Christians learn to defend their faith against heresy. I've shared my testimony more than a hundred times in many different denominations and conferences.

We've attended many "Witnesses Now for Jesus" conferences at Blue Mountain Christian Retreat – a place where former JWs come and enjoy fellowship with others who have found their way out. Blue Mountain has been a place where the presence of the Lord touched our soul. This conference was a place where we heard the real Truth (Jesus) preached. It was also a place where former Mormons as well as JWs could become deprogrammed, unraveling the "*different gospel*."

Presently Bill and I are experiencing our golden years – yes they are golden in that we're fortunate to have many good Christian friends in a church well grounded in the Bible (Hill-n-Dale Christian Church). We're fortunate that our two children are strong Christians as are their spouses. We're blessed to have six grandchildren who are all born again and living out their faith. Bill and I are truly grateful of how the Lord has shown us the way — the truth — and the life! (John 14:6)

APPENDICES

APPENDIX A

Important U.S. documents concerning Christianity

The following are a few direct quotes taken from the historical records that were made by the founders of our nation. These quotes document our national roots. They also document U.S. historical dependency upon Divine Law as the basis of National law and bear testimony of those who have gone before us who strongly believed that the Bible is exactly what it claims to be – the Inspired Divine Revelation of God our Creator from whom all human rights and freedoms are a gift and not bestowed by a king or government.

■ PRESIDENTS

On October 3, 1789, George Washington, the first president and father of our Country in proclaiming a National Day of Prayer and Thanksgiving said, "It is the duty of all nations to acknowledge the Providence of Almighty God, to obey His will, to be grateful for His benefits, and to humbly implore His protection and favor." *[Commander-in-Chief in the American Revolution; Signer of the Constitution; First President of the United States]*

In 1756, John Adams, one of America's founding fathers and its second president, said, "Suppose a nation in some distant region should take the Bible for their only Law Book, and every member should regulate his conduct by the precepts there exhibited...What a paradise would this region be!" *[Signer of the constitution; Fourth President of the United States]*

In 1781, Thomas Jefferson said, "God who gave us life gave us liberty. And can the liberties of a nation be thought secure when we have removed their only firm basis, a conviction in the minds of the people that these liberties are a gift of God? That they are not to be violated but with His wrath? Indeed, I tremble for my country when I reflect that God is just; that His justice cannot sleep forever." *[Signer and the principal author of the Declaration of Independence; Third President of the United States]*

■ FOUNDING FATHERS

Patrick Henry said, "An appeal to arms and to the God of hosts is all that is left us!... Sir, we are not weak if we make a proper use of those means which the God of nature hath placed in our power... Besides, sir, we shall not fight our battles alone. There is a just God who presides over the destinies of nations and who will raise up friends to fight our battles for us... Is life so deaf or peace so sweet as to be purchased at the price of chains and slavery? Forbid it, Almighty God! I know not what course others may take; but as for me, give me liberty or give me death!!!" *[Patriot and Statesman]*

Jedediah Morse said, "To the kindly influence of Christianity we owe that degree of civil freedom, and political and social happiness, which mankind now enjoys... Whenever the pillars of Christianity shall be overthrown, our present republican forms of government – and all blessings which flow from them – must fall with them." *[Patriot and Educator called "The Father of American Geography"]*

■ SUPREME COURT JUSTICES

John Jay - The Bible is the best of all books, for it is the word of God and teaches us the way to be happy in this world and in the next. Continue therefore to read it and to regulate your life by its precepts. *[Co-author of the Federalist Papers; First Chief-Justice of the U.S. Court]*

Joseph Story – One of the beautiful boasts of our municipal jurisprudence is that Christianity is a part of the Common Law... There never has been a period in which the Common Law did not recognize Christianity as lying at its foundations... I verily believe Christianity necessary to the support of civil society. *[U.S Supreme Court Justice, "Father of American Jurisprudence," Placed on the Court by President James Madison]*

■ CONGRESS

"We are a Christian people... not because the law demands it, not to gain exclusive benefits or to avoid legal disabilities, but from choice and education; and in a land thus universally Christian, what is to be expected, what desired, but that we shall pay due regard to Christianity?" *[Senate Judiciary Committee Report, January 19, 1853]*

"At the time of the adoption of the Constitution and the amendments, the universal sentiment was that Christianity should be encouraged... In this age there can be no substitute for Christianity. . .That was the religion of the founders of the republic and they expected it to remain the religion of their descendants." *[House Judiciary Committee Report, March 27, 1854]*

Education
"Let every student be plainly instructed and earnestly pressed to consider well the main end of his life and studies is to know God and Jesus Christ which is eternal Life (John 17.3) and therefore to lay Christ in the bottom as the only foundation of all sound knowledge and learning. And seeing the Lord only giveth wisdom, let every one seriously set himself by prayer in secret to seek it of Him (Proverbs 2,3). Every one shall so exercise himself in reading the Scriptures twice a day that he shall be ready to give such an account of the proficiency therein." *[Harvard – 1636 Student Guidelines]*

"All the scholars are required to live a religious and blameless life according to the rules of God's Word, diligently reading the Holy Scriptures, that fountain of Divine light and truth, and constantly attending all the duties of religion." *[Yale – 1787 Student Guidelines]*

Foreigners
The Americans combine the notions of Christianity and of liberty so intimately in their minds that it is impossible to make them conceive the one without the other. Upon my arrival in the United States, the religious aspect of the country was the first thing that struck my attention; and the longer I stayed there, the more did I perceive the great political consequences resulting from this state of things, to which I was unaccustomed. In France I had almost always seen the spirit of religion and the spirit of freedom pursuing courses diametrically opposed to each other; but in America I found that they were intimately united, and that they reigned in common over the same country. *[Alexis De Tocqueville – French observer of America in 1831, author of Democracy in America.]*

APPENDIX B

The calendar

What single event in human history had the power to split time? The birth of Christ was so significant that virtually the entire world has restarted its calendar because of it. Who is this Christ and why is He so special? The Bible says He is Jesus, the Son of the living God. His birth is so powerful that we now date time from His birth. The 2000 millennium was a milestone – a celebration that makes us even more aware of the impact of Jesus upon our world. If this event had not happened time would not be counted as BC and AD (before and after Christ).

The masthead of the *Jerusalem Post* always carries three dates. On October 15, 1999, it also gave the dates of Heshvan 5, 5760, and 5 Rajab 1420. The first is the Western date; the second is the Jewish date; the third is the Islamic date. Which, if any, is correct, and does it really matter? Understanding the development of our calendars will enable us to realize that the "Christ event" is not in question, it is the differences in calendars. For an informative discussion on these three different calendars and how tracking time relates to the Scriptures, see www.lamblion.com.

APPENDIX C

Believe in Jesus

What does the word "believes" mean in John 3:16, *"For God so loved the world that he gave his one and only Son, that whoever believes in him shall not perish but have eternal life?"*

In context of verse 16, THAYER'S GREEK LEXICON says: "Used especially of the faith by which a man embraces Jesus – a conviction full of joyful trust that Jesus is the Messiah, divinely appointed author of eternal salvation in the Kingdom of God, conjoined with obedience to Christ, rest our faith relationship of Christ with God and close ethical intimacy with him...that therefore not a single thing can happen, not even a sparrow can fall which does not, in the final analysis, serve our best eternal interests."

"Believing" that Jesus is the Son of God has a far greater significance than mere intellectual knowledge. It means we desire to **"know"** Christ Jesus and actually fellowship with Him, as I Jo. 1:3 says, *"....and our fellowship is with the Father and with his Son, Jesus Christ."* (emphasis ours)

Heart knowledge verses intellectual knowledge

The word "believe" in John 3 does not have the same meaning as "believe" in James 2:18, 19: *"But someone will say, 'You have faith, and I have works.' Show me your faith without your works, and I will show you my faith by my works. You believe that there is one God. You do well. Even the demons believe – and tremble!"* The word *"believe"* here, means intellectual knowledge. The demons know who God is, but they certainly don't have a relationship with Him.

Whoever the president of our country may be – we believe it because we know he was elected – but we don't know him personally. It is simply a known fact, or intellectual knowledge. We don't have a personal relationship with him. But when we come to the point in our lives, where we truly believe Jesus is the Son of God, (heart knowledge) we begin our relationship with Him, and then we can repent of all our sins and start a new life in Christ. Repenting means to stop practicing sin and turn around – make a conscious effort to live a life pleasing to God. By reading the Bible, we learn how to please God. Things always go better when we do our best to please Him (Isaiah 48:17-18).

APPENDIX D

God's Name

The revealing of His name was done personally by God Almighty Himself, as HE spoke to the prophet Moses. Moses was preparing to go before Pharaoh to lead the Israelites out of Egypt. Exodus 3:13 and 14 records, "Then Moses said to God, *"Behold I am going to the sons of Israel, and I shall say to them, "The God of your fathers has sent me to you" Now they may say to me, "What is His Name? What shall I say to them." And God said to Moses, "I AM WHO I AM"* and He said, *"Thus you shall say to the sons of Israel, "I AM has sent me to you."*

Notice that in direct response to the question, "What is your name?" God said to Moses, "Thus you shall say "I AM" has sent me unto you." God first gave Moses a name he could "say" or "speak," and then He proceeded to give him another name. Read on to verse 15 of Exodus chapter three. "And God furthermore said to Moses, 'Thus you shall say to the sons of Israel, the LORD (YHWH), the God of Abraham, the God of Isaac, and the God of Jacob has sent me unto you." In providing the two names, God concludes: *"THIS is MY NAME forever, and this is My memorial-name to all generations."*

No person apparently did say the second revealed name of God, for it is the four consonants YHWH. It has no vowels [A,E,I,O,U] which are necessary for speech. The Israelites got around this by writing "YHWH," but when reading scriptures aloud, they said "ADONAI" or "LORD", and many Bibles today put in "LORD" in all capitals to signify the translation of "YHWH". There is no evidence that any attempt to pronounce "YHWH" was ever made by the Israelites, the early church, or by Jesus Christ.

What about "Jehovah"? Some people in recent years have used the name "JEHO-VAH" in place of "YHWH." Some scholars recognize that this "patched-up" name of God invented a mere 700 years ago, with the vowels from "ADONAI" inserted between the consonants "YHWH" and then further altered with the letters, "J" and "V," is incorrect.

In addition to revealing His name as the "I AM" and "YHWH," God also tells us that His name is "JEALOUS" [Exodus 34:14], and " HOLY" [Isaiah 57:15].

SALVATION IN GOD'S NAME

The Psalmist cried out, *"Save me O GOD, by thy NAME!"* [Psalm 54:1], and also, *"Help us, O GOD of our Salvation, for the Glory of thy NAME, and deliver us and forgive our sins for Thy NAME'S sake."* [Psalm 79:9].   YHWH stated in Isaiah 43:11, *"There is no Savior besides ME."* In Zechariah 12:10, YHWH prophesied that *"they will look upon Me whom they have pierced."* In Zechariah 11:12,13, YHWH revealed that HE HIMSELF would be sold for 30 pieces of silver. YHWH further promised that one day He would be King over all the earth and that His name would be the only one. [Zechariah 14:9] How would this come about? The Virgin Mary was told that, *"Behold the Virgin shall be with Child, and shall bear a Son, and they shall call his name 'Emmanuel,' which translated means 'GOD WITH US."* [Matthew 1:23].

Jesus, whose name means "YHWH'S SALVATION," had come! Jesus revealed to the Jews that HE was the "I AM," taking the memorial NAME of God to all generations, and applying it to HIMSELF! (John 8:58). (http://mmoutreachinc.com/index.html)

APPENDIX E

Firstborn

According to Thayer's Greek Lexicon, the word "firstborn" in Colossians 1:15 is translated from the Greek word, "prototokos" (prw/toj, h, on first; leading, foremost, prominent, most important).This passage does not with certainty prove that Paul reckoned 'firstborn' in the number of created beings." Jesus had no beginning (Hebrews 7:4).

The people of Israel attached unusual value to the *firstborn* son and assigned special privileges and responsibilities to him. The *firstborn* son was presented to the Lord when he was a month old. The birthright of a *firstborn* son included a double portion of the estate and leadership of the family after the father's death. The firstborn son customarily cared for his mother until her death and provided for his sisters until their marriage among other things. He held a position of *superiority in privilege* and *authority*.

Therefore, we can easily understand how the word firstborn came to mean, *"a title of position* or *right to rule."*

The *firstborn* might sell his rights as Esau did (Gen 25:29-34) or forfeit them for misconduct as Reuben did for incest (Gen.35:22; 49:3-4).

An example of the use of this term firstborn is seen in the case of David, who was the youngest (eighth) son of Jesse (I Sam.16:10-13) yet referred to in Ps. 89:27 as *firstborn*. Why was David referred to as firstborn? David was king of Israel, thus possessing, *'the right to rule'* and the term firstborn denoted *his status and character* rather than his status as the *firstborn* son of his father Jesse. He was the superior or greater of Jesse's sons.

For a second example see (Gen. 41:51-52).   Manasseh is Joseph's *firstborn* son and Ephraim his second son. Ephraim, Joseph's second born son is said to be the *'firstborn' the one superior / greater* than his brother (Jeremiah.31:9). You may recall the story in Gen. 48:13-20 - Manasseh loses his birthright to Ephraim.   This happened when Israel, Joseph's father, was on his death bed. Israel was "pronouncing blessing," on his grandchildren, Joseph's sons.

APPENDIX F

John 1:1

John 1:1 says, *"In the beginning was the Word, and the Word was with God, and the Word was God."* We wonder how can Jesus be with God and yet be God? We cannot completely comprehend the infinite God with our finite minds. No wonder the whole early church exclaimed in common confession "great is the mystery of godliness" in 1 Timothy 3:16. We must either accept God's revelation of Himself to us, or we end up with unsatisfactory, man-made doctrines.

Some translations change "God" in John 1:1, to "a god," but this is a distortion of God's word. Just because there is a "mystery" surrounding the God-head, this doesn't mean we cannot have correct knowledge concerning God, and in particular, Jesus Christ. Colossians 2:2 tells us to, *"...attain to all the wealth that comes from the full assurance of understanding, resulting in a true knowledge of God's mystery, that is, Christ Himself."* True knowledge is possible and desirable.

Is Jesus called "God" in Scripture? The answer is a resounding "YES!" from all reliable Bible translations. The Angel announcing Jesus' birth said, *"Behold the Virgin shall be with Child, and shall bear a Son, and they shall call His name "Immanuel", which translated means, "God with us"* (Matthew 1:23).

The disciples believed Jesus to be God. Thomas exclaimed to the risen Christ, "My Lord and my God" (John 20:28, 29). Jesus blessed him for saying this. The Apostle Paul admonished the elders in Acts 20:28 *"to shepherd the church of God which He purchased with His own blood,"* proving that Jesus was indeed, God Incarnate.

GOD THE SON: We now call the Father, Yahweh, God, as a witness to His Son's identity. The Father says in Hebrews 1:8, *"But of the Son He says, "Thy Throne, O God, is forever and ever."* If the Father calls the Son "God" (Ho Theos, "THE GOD" in Greek.) I choose to believe it. Jesus Christ is called the "true God" in 1 John 5:20, so we won't make the mistake of believing He is some kind of "extra god." Let's consider the Scripture, *"And we know that the Son of God has come, and has given us understanding, in order that we might know Him who is true, and we are in Him who is true, in His Son Jesus Christ. This is the true God and eternal life."* So far, we have looked at Scriptures calling Jesus, "God," and "the true God," and now we will move on to one that calls Him the "only God." 1 Timothy 1:16.17 says of Jesus Christ, *"And yet for this reason I found mercy, in order that in me as the foremost, Jesus Christ might demonstrate His perfect patience as* an example for those who would believe in Him for eternal life. Now to the King eternal, immortal, invisible, the only God, be honor and glory forever and ever. Amen." Jesus Christ is eternal, with no beginning and no end. He is God, the true God, the only God.

ALMIGHTY GOD: Jesus Christ is in fact called, "Almighty God" in the book of Revelation. Let's read Revelation 1:8, *"I am the Apha and the Omega, says the Lord God, who is and who was and who is to come, the Almighty."* Who's coming? The Almighty! Can we make further identification of the Alpha and Omega? Yes, for in Revelation, chapter 22 the Speaker keeps promising "I am coming quickly." In verse 13 He identifies Himself with the words, *"I am the Alpha and the Omega, the first and the last, the beginning and the end..."* In verse 16, He is more specific, saying, *"I, Jesus, have sent My angel to testify to you these things for the churches."* Verse 20 concludes, *"He who testifies to these things says, "Yes, I am coming quickly." Amen. Come, Lord Jesus."*

Revelation chapter 1, beginning in verse 13, gives a vision of a "son of man", which incidentally is a title of Jesus Christ. In verse 17 and 18, we read these words, *"I am the first and the last, and the living One; and I was dead, and behold, I am alive forevermore, and I have the keys of death and of Hades."* So the "Alpha and Omega" is the First and the Last.

This Son of Man, this Jesus, is the only one who died and rose again and conquered death. He gives Himself the Revelation titles, "Alpha and Omega," "the First and the Last," and, of course, "Almighty God."

The late Dr. Walter Martin, probably the foremost expert on the cults in the world, and a renowned bible scholar, gives this true definition of the Trinity: *"Within the unity of the One God there are three Persons, the Father, the Son, and the Holy Spirit; and these three share the same Nature and attributes. In effect then, the three Persons are the One God."* (http://mmoutreachinc.com/index.html)

APPENDIX G

Church – Church Age

Church is the term most frequently used in the New Testament to describe a group of people professing faith and trust in Jesus Christ. Beginning with the Apostles, Christians have met to worship Him and have continually encouraged others to become His followers. The early Christians understood themselves as *'the people'* of the *'God who had revealed Himself''* in the Old Testament (Heb.1:1-2). Following Jesus is not simply about forgiveness, it is also about transformation, becoming like Jesus (2 Cor.3:18). We have the ability to become more like Him. Followers of Jesus live under the influence of the Holy Spirit abiding in them.

The most prominent characteristic of the church is devotion to the Messiah, Jesus Christ, as **Lord**. Jesus taught His disciples that His followers would continue making disciples until His return. (Matt.28:18-20; John 14:12-14). This period of time is known as "the church age." Just as "the church age" began in a spectacular manner the conclusion will also be supernatural and spectacular.

Three specific events in the life of the Messiah, Jesus, were prerequisites to establish the Church:

1. Jesus' death by which the atonement for sin was provided
   (Matt.16:18-21),
2. His resurrection (see Eph.1:20-23), and
3. His ascension (Eph.4:7-11). The Holy Spirit was not given until
   after Christ's ascension.

The Church was born on the day of Pentecost when 'the Holy Spirit was manifested'. This event was celebrated with miraculous signs and wonders appropriate for such an awesome occasion (Acts 2:1-12). On this day, the resurrected Lord Jesus Christ, from His position of authority in heaven as Head of the Church, joined all believers, Jew and Gentile (Eph.3:1-12) into one body and placed them in the care and safekeeping of the Holy Spirit during their time on earth (I Cor. 12:13). The entrance into the body of Christ is by Spirit-baptism. The Church is the body of Christ (Col.1:18).

Members of the church were 'set apart' to demonstrate the power of Christ's redemption in their own lives by changed conduct (Rom.12:1-13:7; Col.3:12-4:1). The overcoming of sinful behavior in the lives of Christians was/is a witness or testimony to the redeeming power of Christ (Gal.5:22-26). The sins of people were clearly identified (Gal. 5:19-21). Christians were expected to adopt a new way of life that was appropriate to their commitment to Christ (Eph.4:17-24).

Worship in the early church demonstrated the lordship of Christ, not only because He was worshiped and praised, but also because worship demonstrated the obligation of Christians to love and to nurture one another (Heb. 10:25). The church is seen as the body of Christ:

- Jesus is the head (Eph. 4:15-16)
- the members are the body or bride
  (1 Cor. 6:12-20; 12:12-27; Eph.5:22-31)
- new creation (2 Cor. 5:17; Eph. 2:14-15)
- stand against Satan (Eph. 6:10-20)
- salt and light (Matt.5:13-16)
- saints (1 Cor. 1:2),
- faithful witnesses (Col. 1:2; John 15:26-27),
- household of God (1 Pet. 4:17),
- brethren (brothers and sisters in Christ; I Cor.14:26).

APPENDIX H

GNOSTICISM
(Notes from NIV Study Bible in part)

One of the most dangerous heresies of the first two centuries of the church was Gnosticism. Gnosticism was a popular belief that threatened the very foundation of Christianity. Some teachers were attempting to blend Gnosticism with Christianity. *(Forms of Gnosticism still exist today under different names).* When people choose to hold to their particular philosophy and adopt portions of Biblical truth the results are false teaching or heresy. (Heresy is a view at variance with the truths of the Scriptures that misleads, produces dissension and schisms within the church and confuses others.)

By the time of the Council of Carthage 397 A.D., a great volume of commentary on the scriptures had been produced. The letter of the Apostle Paul to the Colossians and I, II, and III John by the Apostle John are letters / books identifying who Jesus is and refuting Gnostic teaching about Jesus. Acquaintance with early Gnosticism is also reflected in I and II Timothy, Titus and II Peter and perhaps I Corinthians.

Gnosticism's central teaching was that spirit (soul, angels, God) is entirely good and matter (flesh, the world) is entirely evil.

1. Man's body, which is matter, is therefore evil. Gnostics believed their soul to be good and their body to be evil.

2. Salvation was found through <u>escaping the body</u>, for it was believed that man is basically a good spirit trapped inside an evil body. Salvation could be achieved <u>not by faith in Christ</u> but <u>by special knowledge</u>. Gnostics taught that obtaining *certain higher knowledge* rather than faith in Christ was the key to salvation. *(The Greek word for "knowledge" is gnosis, hence Gnosticism).*

   The problem: How did these people who accepted Jesus get around the fact that Jesus (God) came in evil flesh and yet was pure, holy and sinless?

3. Christ's true humanity was denied in two ways by Gnostics:
   (1) Some said that Jesus only seemed to have a physical body and kept the idea that He was good, pure and holy. These people became known

as *Docetics*, taken from the Greek term *'dokein'* meaning '<u>to seem.</u>' *(James White in his book, "The Forgotten Trinity," said, " Docetics would tell stories about Jesus and a disciple walking by the seashore, talking about the mysteries of the kingdom. At some point the disciple would turn around and look back upon their path and discover that there was only one set of footprints. Why? Because Jesus doesn't leave footprints, since He only 'seemed to' have a physical body.")*

(2) Others said that the divine Christ joined the man Jesus at baptism and left Him before He died, a view called *Cerinthianism* after its most prominent spokesman, *Cerinthus.*

This dualism led to two extremes of behavior.

A. Some became ascetics, depriving themselves by fasts and monastic living even to the point of forbidding marriage. *These groups died out in a couple generations.*

B. Some reasoned that the goal was to escape one's body and the spirit wasn't affected by what the body did, so why not just enjoy practicing extremes of immorality.

4. Paradoxically, this dualism also led to licentiousness. The reasoning was that, since matter and not the breaking of God's law (I John 3:4-6) was considered evil, breaking his law was of no moral consequence.

Understanding Gnosticism explains why the Apostle John in II John 7-10 is addressing this issue. Read v7-10 - This is a reference to the Gnostics, who believed *"that they had advanced beyond the teaching of the apostles."* In v9 John is combating the heresy of the true teaching about Christ as the incarnate God-man. According to v10, one is not welcomed who does not teach in the true personage of Christ. This seems to address the issue of teaching as opposed to one coming in for a mere visit or conversation. John was warning against providing food and lodging for false teachers (Gnostics). Doing so would be an investment in the wicked work of denying the fact that Jesus came in the flesh and give public approval to their lie. *(Ordinarily it was customary to provide a visiting teacher food and lodging).*

TUTORS FOR CHRIST
www.tutorsforchrist.org

To order more books

Bird's Eye View of the Bible

$10 each – add $3.00 for mailing USA

Jean Eason
467 Sandalwood Dr.
Lexington, KY 40505

Bird's-Eye View of the Bible is a great resource for anyone seeking to know more about God and the Christian faith, or as a guide while discipling or witnessing to a friend. This book is a scripturally based work that covers multiple aspects of our faith and how it is lived out historically and in today¹s society.

— Rev. John Edgar Harris
Student Minister & Director of Communications,
Glynwood Baptist Church • Prattville, Alabama

This book is a terrific resource. The testimonies are uplifting, its evangelistic thrust is terrific and the book confronts the growing problem of illiteracy about the faith head on. This is exactly what so many in the Body of Christ desperately need in our day. The book is a superb "nuts and bolts" resource that I feel sure will be used by many. I am so glad to be able to recommend it and to participate in the project.

— Eric Barger, Founder
Take A Stand! Ministries • Rowlett, Texas
www.ericbarger.com

I wish we had this little book when we were first saved! I believe this will be a great tool in helping new believers get grounded in the faith and create a desire for more. This book takes the building blocks of Christianity and makes them simple and understandable.

— Paul Blizard, Senior Pastor
Memorial Baptist Church • Beckley, West Virginia

This is a masterful job! May this be just the tool we need to win and then disciple people for our Lord Jesus. It will be exciting to see how God uses it. It is true, great things come in small packages. This is powerful.

— Dr. Charles Love
Grace Bible Church • Silver Lakes, CA